MARINELL HARRIMAN
HOUSE RABBIT
HANDBOOK
How to Live with an Urban Rabbit

FOURTH EDITION

Drollery Press

To Herman and Phoebe
and their successors

Drollery Press, Alameda
Copyright 1985, 1991, 1995, 2005 by Marinell Harriman
All rights reserved.
First edition published 1985. Second edition 1991, Third edition 1995
Fourth edition 2005
Printed in Peru
15 14 13 12 11 10 9 8 7 6 5 4 3

Cover, Title Page and interior photographs by the author,
plus additional photographs by Amy Espie and others, as noted.

Printing by Quebecor World Latin America.
Design by Bob Harriman

Library of Congress Control Number: 2005900723
ISBN-13: 978-0-940920-17-0
ISBN-10: 0-940920-17-4

Drollery Press
1524 Benton Street
Alameda, California 94501

Contents

Preface

Y OU SURELY KNOW BY NOW that rabbits are worthy creatures. They are demure enough to make us relax and powerful enough to make us rearrange our homes so that they can live there safely. The fourth edition of the *House Rabbit Handbook* no longer needs to introduce the concept of "house rabbit" to a world that is unfamiliar with that term, as it was in 1985. By the second edition, in 1991, word was out that rabbits were "the pet of the 90s." Since that decade has come and gone, the facts remain. House rabbits are not a fad. They are not Easter toys. They are year-round companions to millions of people around the world.

As we have evolved from the third to the fourth edition, we have also made more use of the Internet, as a major means of communication—sharing bunny stories, photos, and information. The *House Rabbit Handbook* now addresses a much more educated and demanding readership than it did in those early days. But while rabbit people are ever pursuing, and contributing to, a more advanced body of information, the basic how-to education is still necessary. We were all beginners at one time.

Over the past 20 years of living with house rabbits, I've discovered a most amazing fact. You don't run out of things to learn. Our bunnies continue to reveal their intricate personalities and social order and teach us to be more observant efficient humans. We humans are constantly developing new and better ways to get our work done so we can enjoy our homes with our bunnies. And to preserve the joy as long as possible, our ears are always open for new breakthroughs in veterinary medicine that might keep our bunnies alive and well for a long time.

ACKNOWLEDGEMENTS

I would like to thank the following contributors for providing valuable information, for reviewing material, and for editing or proofreading:

Sandi Ackerman	Joy Gioia
Susan A. Brown, D.V.M.	Bill Harriman, Ph.D.
Mary Cotter, Ed.D.	Carolynn Harvey, D.V.M.
Susan Davis	Holly O'Meara
Margo DeMello, Ph.D.	Susan Smith, Ph.D.
Amy Espie	Beth Woolbright
George Flentke, Ph.D.	

Thanks also to those who contributed photos and experiences and to the many veterinarians who have donated their time to improve the quality of care for our dearly loved creatures.

I am also grateful to the humane societies and rescue groups that do their best to give the less fortunate bunnies a second chance, as well as all the volunteers who spend countless hours educating people so that rabbits can become cherished family members in the loving homes they so deserve. ∎

Customs and Characteristics

First get acquainted with the general characteristics of the species. Then you can better meet the needs of the individual rabbits who share your home.

Left: *Daphne rabbit finds Tania cat.*
Inset: *Helen Lau with Kappa.*

PHOTOS: ABOVE, AMY ESPIE; INSET, FRANKLIN CHOW

The Mental Makeup

WHAT A GREAT SURPRISE it is to new rabbit people that they have an intelligent creature in their midst with an inquisitive mind that is constantly looking for activity. Rabbits are comprised of paradoxes that make them extremely entertaining—inquisitive yet cautious, skittish yet confident, energetic yet lazy, timid yet bold.

Being crepuscular, not nocturnal, rabbits are most active at dawn and twilight. They spend a long mid-day "down time," during which they usually seek the solitude of a cage or quiet corner for a nap. This habit fits the schedule of working people who are away from home part of the day. Rabbits will adapt well into any consistent human routine.

Living low to the ground (floor, carpet), they are clumsy in high places. Yet, their explorations may take them from inside the closet, behind the sofa, or under the bed to the heights of dressers, desktops, and tables. Solid footing is required for the loftier investigations. A single youthful rabbit can lay waste to the contents of accessible shelves, delighting in pulp fiction and the daily news. And the clatter heard from the kitchen is most likely due to pots and pans being rearranged.

WITTY AND WILY

Rabbits solve problems, like pushing on doors that open outward and pulling with their teeth on doors that open inward. They learn to use a litterbox, to come when they're called, and to sit up and beg for a treat. They have a remarkable ability to remember furniture arrangements and where tasty snacks are usually kept.

They can learn procedures and routines at any age. Smart animals that they are, rabbits play games—with toys, with other animals, and with their humans. They play games of their own invention, punctuated by sudden vertical leaps and 180° turns in mid-air.

Consistent with those of other animals, rabbits' games mimic sur-

High-minded exploration:
Hopping with compulsive curiosity from bed to dresser, Herman stops to reflect.

"...when allowed some freedom, rabbits perform beyond their supposed capacity"

vival techniques. Just as predatory animals enjoy chase games, rabbits more often play getaway games. Sometimes carrying a prized possession (such as a carrot), one may run from imagined thieves. Or after yanking an envelope from a human hand, a frisky rabbit zigzags off with a "catch-me-if-you-can" dare to pursuers. And on many occasions, witnesses have observed rabbits playing follow-the-leader.

AGE OF INNOCENCE

In terms of conforming to human standards of acceptable indoor behavior, a rabbit's age of innocence is at maturity. Most rabbits don't reach their full potential for a relationship with humans until after their first year. By this time too many humans have discarded them.

The stage of intense curiosity, hyperactivity, and frantic chewing and digging occurs at the height of adolescence (4-8 months)—a time that we recommend neutering or spaying. During adolescence, or preferably before, a house rabbit's environment should be thoroughly bunny-proofed, and plenty of litterboxes should be available (details in chapters 4-5).

Some of the rabbits we rescued years ago were never adopted into new homes and have continued to live with us. As they settled in, they became very easy to manage and very mellow. (All are spayed or

Literary pursuits: Elevated taste for stimulating books drive the youthful Trixie beyond the lower shelves of required reading.

neutered.) Our seniors (over 6 years) may move about a little slower and sleep a lot more, but they retain their wonderful personalities and good habits.

FREEDOM TO PERFORM

Like other animals when allowed some freedom, rabbits perform beyond their supposed capacity. The key here is opportunity. What individual expression can you expect from an animal who never gets out of a cage?

One year, we were passing out educational papers at a pet fair. Our booth displayed examples of rabbit toys and a photo collection of house rabbits doing their normal things. A man stopped at our booth and exclaimed, "Wow! I didn't know rabbits could do all of this! Ours is in a hutch in our backyard, and she just sits there."

"Rabbits who live in our houses take up our habits."

Newly enlightened, the man went home to turn his hutch rabbit into a house rabbit, and we celebrated her victory.

Rabbits who live in our houses take up our habits. Like us, they are preoccupied with appearances and are meticulous groomers. They engage in household activities with other occupants. They learn many human words. They can distinguish their name, as well as, "Come," "Box," "Outside," "Yum," "Let's go," and a number of endearing terms and sweet nothings mentioned in the right tone of voice. Rabbits make a big effort to learn our language. It's our turn to learn theirs. ■

Just Routine: *Patrick does some serious ear washing (inset) while Daphne wipes her face in jest (right). Darla's daily ritual is a game with her human.*

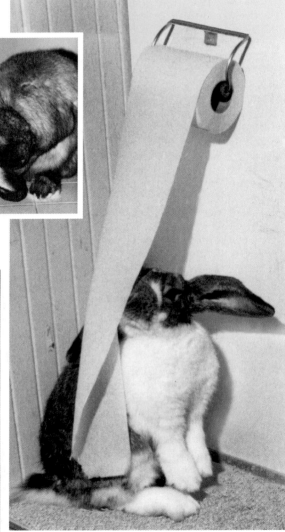

PHOTOS: LEFT, DON LATARSKI; RIGHT, INSET: MARINELL HARRIMAN

Rabbit-Speake

WHEN WE FIRST STARTED to "rabbit school" we learned some basic vocabulary. With time, we are refining our education and even learning a little rabbit poetry along the way.

Scientific observations of wild rabbits give us background data on rabbit behavior. When we live with rabbits, we watch them closeup and listen to what they are saying when they "speak" to humans. In living with different people, rabbits develop different "dialects," which are best understood by those who live with them and love them.

Just as in our own language, we have homonyms (the same word with different meanings) so do rabbits. The important thing to bear in mind is context.

A BODY OF INFORMATION

Most rabbit "words" are communicated by action. Others are transmitted simply by posture. Happy postures include whole-body smiles of several kinds.

The peaceful stretch. Bunny flattens out on his belly with hind feet extended straight out. Upon occasion, toes may curl under, or the feet may cross at the ankles.

The sideways flop. If you find your bunny flopped over on his side or back, it does not mean he has had a heart attack. The fluttering eyelids and whiskers indicate that bunny is contentedly in dreamland.

Presentation, another smile, in the horizontal position, is assumed by the recipient of petting by a favorite human or grooming by

another animal. All feet are tucked under, while the chin is laid out flat on the floor. This is how subordinate rabbits "present" themselves to their superiors. But a presentation is also used as voluntary submission to a loved one, meaning something like: "Take me. I'm yours" (such as Oliver's submission on page 44).

Crouching is an unrelaxed version of presenting, usually with bulging eyes, in which the rabbit is not enjoying attention but rather frozen in fear.

The shudder. This is a comical whole-body expression. If your hands emit an obnoxious odor—like too much perfume or carburetor cleaner—when you pet your bunny, he may try to shake it off. Some-

Lapin laughter *is unmistakable in The Bun's joyful wake-up yawn (left).*
Phoebe's phonetics of the feet *(above) stand for happiness, friendship, comfort, and a general sense of well-being.*

PHOTOS: LEFT, WRENN DABNEY REED; RIGHT, TANIA HARRIMAN

"A rabbit who licks a human hand is not just trying to get salt..."

times after a rabbit is given medicine, he may shake his coat to rid himself of the bad taste.

WORD OF MOUTH

Another "word" with two different definitions is tooth grinding.

Purring. This is a series of fast but light vibrations of the teeth and happily quivering whiskers—activated by gentle stroking behind the ears. It signifies contentment to the Nth degree.

Crunching. The second meaning is one of discomfort, expressed by a sick animal. Tooth crunching is usually a louder slower grind, sometimes with protruding eyes. Context will help you distinguish a happy grind from a painful crunch.

The whimper is a fretting little noise made by a pregnant or pseudo-pregnant female, who is pleading not to be disturbed. Some rabbits whimper when you try to pick them up or pull them from their cage.

Wheezing sniffs. Other rabbits "voice" a protest by combining vocalizations with nasal sounds.

Clucking. A pleasant sound is the faint *clucking* made by a bunny who has been given a particularly tasty snack. It always means, Yum, yum!

LOVE AND WAR

Rabbits are very intense over friends and enemies and use obvious language to address them.

Licking/grooming. This is obvious affection. A rabbit who licks a human hand is not just trying to get salt—as some people who are unfamiliar with rabbit talk may believe. What a silly idea! Rabbits don't lick each other because they crave salt. Rather, they crave affection.

Honking/oinking. Because rabbits draw very little distinction between sexual and social behavior, many expressions are identical. Neutered males and spayed females may still court—circling each other (or your feet). Soft honking or oinking is a love song, also used to solicit food and attention. A honk can mean: I want you, or maybe a treat

Nudging/huddling. More ways to show affection involve sitting close. These friendly gestures are often overlooked by humans. Instead of licking, many house rabbits nuzzle nose-to-nose with their human friends. Nudging your ankle or tugging on your pant-leg means, Notice me.

Nipping. This is not necessarily an angry remark. Happily bonded pairs use it all the time simply to mean, Move over. With humans it sometimes means, I'm scared of heights. Put me down.

Snorting/growling. In anger this may be just a warning or it may coincide with a grunt-lunge-bite directed at an adversary. This kind of anger is predictable and can be prevented (see page 54)

TALL TAILS AND ASSERTIONS

Most of the time you are seeing only the tip of bunny's tail, which looks like a small cotton ball—until something excites her.

Erect tail. The excitement shown by a tall erect tail

Body talk: *Phoebe has sassy words for one cat, yet endearing words for a different cat.*

can be caused by the threat of an adversary, the proximity of a potential lover, anticipation of tasty treats, or simply the appearance of a new toy.

Tail twitching. In a competitive or a courting context, rabbits may twitch their tails from side to side and spray their conquests. A modified assertion is simply tail-twitching as a form of "back talk."

Ear assertions. Ears send and receive messages. Alert *forward ears* say, I hear you. Alert *bi-directional ears* say, I hear you and something else, too.

PHOTOS: TANIA HARRIMAN

Menacing, tightly *pulled back ears* say, Watch out!

Chin assertions. A benignly assertive gesture is chinning, a peculiar way of claiming property. By rubbing their under-chin scent glands on the items, they mark them as possessions(undetectable to us).

FEET NOT ON THE GROUND

In addition to smiling, feet may kick, dance, thump, or take a variety of actions.

Kicking. In protest, kicking is high and to the back. In play or combat, rabbits kick to the side.

"Nature has designed rabbits—through shape and wiliness—to thwart predators."

Dancing. You'll know it when you see this frolicking series of sideways kicks and mid-air leaps accompanied by a few head shakes and body gyrations. Many rabbits have literally danced their way into human affection.

Thumping. This has several meanings: I detect something out of the ordinary, or I have an announcement to make.

Rabbits thump over many things—sights, sounds, smells, and things that we don't sense. It might be a danger signal, and then again it might not be. You might be warned of "danger" that the furniture has been rearranged.

Yet, this sense of propriety is the very thing that can make a rabbit a highly suitable individual to share your home. ∎

Learning from The Experts

By Amy Espie

*W*e humans are a talkative species. Most of our communications are conducted through the written or spoken word. Sharing our lives with rabbits gives us the opportunity to learn a language based more on body position, facial expression and actions. Observation of rabbits conversing with one another provides lessons in grammar and vocabulary as well as in rabbit rules of etiquette.

Rabbits have evolved an enviably simple, direct philosophy: If an experience, event, or behavior is pleasant and rewarding, pursue it; if unpleasant, stressful, or frightening, avoid it. Convoluted motivations such as spite or revenge are refreshingly absent. When a rabbit has a grievance, she's not shy to air it. When Daisy's partner gets between Daisy and a slice of banana, she immediately and clearly corrects him for this gaffe. She doesn't waste time sulking or plotting revenge when a simple, sudden, and well-aimed nip is so much more effective. With few lessons, Milo learns to place himself on the far side of the banana.

Daisy and Milo demonstrate two basic elements of training— timing and association. Rabbits know that in training, timing is all. At the exact instant when Daisy wants Oscar to get out of the way, she nips him.

This explains why a squirt of water in the face of rabbits who are fighting makes sense. It's short and sharp and immediately produces the desired response. Similarly, a handful of hay placed in one corner of the litterbox provides a perfectly timed reward for anyone who happens to hop in.

If the sight of her carrier always signals a trip to the vet, then we are using the power of association to (inadvertently) train Daisy to run and hide whenever she sees the carrier. If, on the other hand, the carrier is a place where she regularly finds a tasty treat and a welcoming rug, we are helping to minimize the stress of travel. In addition, since we know that stress contributes to illness, we can think of this as a health-maintenance exercise.

Of course rabbits have memory just as we do, but they also are blessed with the ability to live very much in the present moment. When they're angry, they fight. When they're happy, they grind their teeth. They don't harbor long-simmering grudges. If you're looking for role models in your effort to be here now, look no further. ∎

Amy Espie is editor of the House Rabbit Journal's Behavior Department and a photo contributor since 1988.

Herman's Place

HERMAN WAS A GIRL. The fact that we named her Herman should give you some idea how little we knew about rabbits (e.g., how to determine their gender) when she hopped into our yard in 1981. By the time we discovered our error, she had learned her name, which suited her just fine.

I have told Herman's story so many times that you might think the computer has hung up. Yet, I have come to realize that Herman is a symbol. She is the experience that changed the way many people think of rabbits. Letters from all over the world relive this experience—of the first rabbit and human ignorance that turned into knowledge. "This was my Herman," I am reading on the backs of enclosed photos.

When we first met Herman, my husband assumed he would build a hutch in the backyard, but we would keep her in the kitchen until then. The hutch was never built.

During our house takeover, we held another crazy notion—that our bedroom was not a bunny room. We had not reckoned with a rabbit who could open doors and sneak into our bedroom and become so exhilarated over her victory that she would turn our bed into a trampoline. Amused, we let her have it during the day. We continued to put her in the kitchen at night, while she continued to insist on sleeping with us. It took another six months before she won. We had to adjust to having our faces licked every ten minutes all through the night. It did occur to me to turn over, but I would usually find that she was standing on my hair (all fourteen pounds of her) and had me pinned to the pillow.

FAIR AND PROPER TREATMENT

Herman demonstrated a remarkable sense of fairness in the equal distribution of petting, grooming, and licking. She would shove her head under Bob's hand when it was his turn to pet her. I can't claim that she actually counted, but after a given number of strokes, it was her turn to groom him again.

Animals are not necessarily child substitutes. Sometimes it's the other way around. Herman was often a parent, or a grandparent. She may not have wiped away tears with her apron, but she could certainly soothe and comfort us and assure us that things were OK.

In seeing that things were properly done, Herman supervised all household activities from fixing

the washer to sorting out magazines. Propriety could be mixed with mischief, as newspapers were grabbed from startled readers' hands. It soon became apparent, after we chased her around the room, that it was the attention she wanted, not the paper. "You cheat," I often told her. "You manipulate me with your charms, and it's not fair."

At times she was downright sneaky, revealing her guilt with her tail. I might have walked by her unaware that she had pulled a book from the bookshelf, until I saw her tail twitching defiantly.

A SENSE OF HUMOR

I was taken by surprise when Herman accepted my invitation to play. I crouched down and wiggled my fingers ghoulishly and said, "I'm going to *get* you." With that information, she kicked up her heels and playfully flung her huge frame from side to side for the whole

Ecstasy of two kinds: After a hard day's work, Herman indulges in total relaxation (left) or an extra helping of parsley from her drawer (right).

length of our living room, leaving me in gaping astonishment. "She gets it!" I said. "She really gets it!"

MEANINGFUL LIVES

Because her time with us was short, only two and a half years, we had to find out why. In the course of learning better rabbit-care, we have met many other people who are motivated by the same kind of loss and work toward the same goals. In tribute to these wonderful rabbits who have determined our cause, we seek improvements in the quality of life for the others of their kind.

Herman's place in "rabbit history" is that of catalyst in a "movement" that demands consideration, respect and quality care for rabbits. Without Herman there would be no *House Rabbit Handbook,* and there would be no House Rabbit Society and many of the other organizations that rescue rabbits and educate people across the country. The door that Herman opened stays open as long as her work is being done and people's hearts are being captured. ∎

PHOTOS: BOB HARRIMAN

Preparing to Adopt

After making your selection, plan a get-acquainted session in an observation circle, where humans can watch bunny, and bunny can investigate humans.

Left: Teddy and Lilac try out Bill and Amy Harriman's family—Aladdin, Nico, and Rian.
Inset: Joyce Haven with Celeste

PHOTOS: ABOVE, BOB HARRIMAN; INSERT, TANIA HARRIMAN

Family Planning

HUMAN BEHAVIOR IS FAR MORE IMPORTANT than rabbit behavior in a rewarding human-rabbit friendship. Instead of insisting that your new housemate meet all of your needs, concentrate on learning about and meeting your bunny's needs.

YOUR QUALIFICATIONS

Before deciding what kind of bunny you want, think about the kind of home you are offering. If it is an empty house all day, think in terms of adopting a

Bonding pen at the HRS Rabbit Center provides a place for Kirby (with spots) to get acquainted with Princess while his humans, Kelli Jimenez and Matt Davis, supervise the introduction.

bonded pair and test yourself to see if you qualify to live with one or more of these deserving animals:

Sense of humor. Do you have it?

Rabbit language. Are you willing to watch, listen to, and learn it?

Home decor. Are you willing to make some compromises in your furniture arrangement?

Vacuuming. Are you willing to do a little more than you would in a rabbit-less home?

Supervision. Are you willing to supervise other animals and children's activities with the rabbit?

Safe environment. Are you willing to provide it?

Relocation. Are you willing to take your bunny with you when you change your residence?

Veterinary care. Are you willing to get treatment when your bunny is sick?

If you qualify in those areas, that's a good start. Willingness must be present on your part before you can make your home a suitable place for a rabbit.

CHOOSING A RABBIT

A preconceived notion of the desired breed, size, and age will exclude some wonderful possibilities. Breed purity and youth are not prerequisites for a marvelous companion, and litterbox training is even easier with an older neutered rabbit, who has settled into a routine.

Considerations should have more to do with your lifestyle than with aesthetics, and the "right" rabbit for you can be any one who would be happy in your home. (There may be more than one.) Too much emphasis on the right rabbit may lead you to believe, at the first difficulty, that you have chosen the wrong rabbit. Or worse yet, you may blame the rabbit for not fitting your expectations. This can happen when you are trying to replace one you have lost. Every rabbit needs to be appreciated for his or her own intrinsic virtues.

Special considerations do, however, need to be made in selecting a friend for another rabbit. Personality may be important here, but not size. Age is an issue only in meeting differing exercise needs in "May-December" matches. Since second adoptions are welcome at most shelters, the staff will often help with the matchmaking. If a bonding pen is available and all rabbits are neutered/spayed, adopters can bring in their first rabbit to choose his or her own companion. The bonding session may result in an unexpected partner, but the humans usually defer to the choice made by their bunny.   *(continued on 18)*

Shelter Work

BY BETH WOOLBRIGHT

WANTED: Bunny with an adorable face who acts like a real rabbit.

UNWANTED: Bunny with an adorable face who acts like a real rabbit

Every day, rabbits are turned into shelters around the world, their owners unable—or unwilling—to continue to care for them. It used to be the highest rate of surrender came in the months after Easter with the "Easter rejects"—as Easter babies grew into rascally adolescents. But now the surrenders are year-round. After cats and dogs, rabbits are the third most common animals at most shelters in the United States. Other reasons given for giving up a bunny include allergies; "no time"; "didn't know the rabbit would live so long"; "kids outgrew 'it'"; "tired of watching him live alone in a corner of the garage"; "didn't meet breed standards."

Usually rabbits in shelters and humane societies face a gamble of

time. Most shelters are open access, which means they take in every animal in need, and there's a limit to how much time they provide each animal. A not unusual result: euthanasia. (Abandoning a bunny in the wild can have even more tragic results, with the chances of predators or starvation.) But shelters also provide warmth and care, veterinary attention and attention from volunteers. Sometimes it's the most attention a rabbit has received in months. Bonuses for adopters come in the form of the rabbit already being spayed or neutered, perhaps a

microchip (in case of getting lost), bunny matchmaking services (for those who've been spayed or neutered), and rabbits who've already been socialized.

Some nonprofit rescue groups, such as House Rabbit Society, work directly with shelters to provide foster care for bunnies who run out of time at the shelter. They take care of rabbits until permanent homes can be found. At shelters and foster homes, volunteers play a crucial role in caring for these precious animals: cleaning litter-boxes and habitats, providing grooming and toys, sitting on the floor and socializing, and letting the bunnies act like real rabbits, so they know how special they are.

For the first-time adopter or a seasoned rabbit person, where's the place to get a rabbit? A shelter or rescue group. Want to enjoy the company of more bunnies than just your own? They're a great place for you to volunteer. ∎

Beth Woolbright *is a supervisor at the Rabbit Center and editor of House Rabbit Journal's Letters Department.*

PHOTO OF BETH WOOLBRIGHT BY MARINELL HARRIMAN

"Parents have the ultimate responsibility for happiness in the home…"

Gentle offering: Bruno pauses from play to accept a carrot.
Quiet time: (opposite page) Harrison, Bruno, and Phoebe Brand.

THE PERFECT HOUSEHOLD

Creating the ideal rabbit home with humans of mixed ages requires the following ingredients: 1) Well behaved children—all the time, 2) Vigilant parents—all the time, and 3) Bunnies who love to be fondled, hugged, and patted—all the time. The reality is that the first ingredient seldom exists, and the third does not exist. That leaves only the second ingredient to make the idealization into reality. Parents have the ultimate responsibility for happiness in the home, as well as the opportunity to contribute to a truly better world.

LONG-TERM PLANS

If you are considering adopting a bunny into a home where there already are or soon will be children under 7 years old, plan on working with both rabbits and children; or postpone the bunny adoption until the children are older. Plans should always include a safe place for the bunny to retreat to when he tires of the children's activities. For the rabbit, size can be an advantage. Parents often think they want a small bunny whom their children can pick up. A far better choice, especially if the family includes toddlers, is a rabbit with some heft that the kids cannot pick up. Parents don't expect children to pick up and carry the family dog. Why pick up the family rabbit?

A useful guide for parents can be downloaded from <www.rabbit.org/kids/faq/Teaching Children to be Rabbit People> by Carolyn Mixon, of Austin, Texas. In it she gives the following advice:

Rabbit behavior/language. Learn so you can point out the rabbit's feelings about your child's actions.

Inappropriate child behavior. Anticipate and prevent it by setting up situations for success.

Reprimands. Avoid situations that require them. The most effective reprimand is to keep the child away from the rabbit for a short time.

Praise. Be generous with praise when the child is gentle with and respectful of the rabbit.

A closed off room. Put the rabbit in it when there are lots of young guests.

Children's friends. Only when 1 or 2 friends visit, show them where the rabbit lives and how to pet. Never leave children unsupervised with the bunny.

DEALING WITH THE UNPLANNED

It's always best to make decisions in advance when expanding your family with both human and non-human members. But sometimes you might be called upon to open your mind and heart to the unexpected. If you should so happen upon a stray rabbit who needs a home, try working backwards and educate yourself in rabbit care. You may have found a precious treasure, planned or not. ∎

Big Bunnies, Big Hearts
By SUSAN DAVIS

We weren't planning on getting a third rabbit the day we met Bruno. In fact, my two children and I felt quite blessed with our existing menagerie: two rabbits, two mice, and two fish. But when we walked into the House Rabbit Society Rabbit Center one sunny afternoon and saw Bruno lolling contentedly in his cage, our hearts flip flopped.

It might have been the huge ears that turned gracefully in our direction as we greeted him. It might have been the giant back feet. Or perhaps it was his kind expression as he gazed at my kids, a look that seemed to say, "Well you're awfully short for humans. Do you know how to pat?" Whatever it was, my five-year-old daughter looked up at me eagerly and said, "Can we get him, Mom? Please?"

Parents hear this question from children all the time and it's important to respond to it with care. Children are a lot of work. Pets are a lot of work. I love having

children and pets, but I'm deeply committed to keeping my collection of both at a sustainable level. Moreover, our young mini-Rex, Spotty, had never bonded with Maybelline, our senior, rabbit. If we were to get a third bunny, we'd have to be absolutely sure that he'd enjoy our lively family, including Maybelline. I could handle three rabbits, but only if at least two of them got along.

So I gave my daughter the classic Mommy response: "Maybe."

One advantage of getting a rabbit from the House Rabbit Society is that the guardians know the rabbits personally. After asking the shelter staff about Bruno's temperament (operative word: "peach"), we put him in a pen with the children.

He promptly stretched out between them and fell asleep with his chin on my daughter's shin. The matter was settled. A few days later, after shelter staff helped us bond Bruno and Maybelline, we brought him home.

Some people who come to our house are a little nervous about Bruno. Big bunnies just look scarier than small bunnies. But although Bruno on his hind legs is as tall as my four-year-old son, he is by far the gentlest, calmest rabbit I've ever met, especially around children. That makes him the perfect family pet. But by bringing home a third rabbit we've also learned, yet again, that different animals have different personalities and needs— that a rabbit like Spotty needs quiet places to hide, and a rabbit like Maybelline needs not to picked up, while a rabbit like Bruno truly lives for carrots, pats, and compliments. That's a crucial life lesson for children and adults alike. ∎

Susan Davis *is a freelance writer and co-author of* STORIES RABBITS TELL. *She and her family live in Alameda, California.*

Adequate Hop-About Time

Before you bring your first bunny into your home, consider bunny's living space and running space. Your bunny can get by with a roomy condo for resting time, but what about playtime?

Bunny needs to stretch his legs, jump, dance, and explore. If you can't spend four hours per day supervising your bunny's activities, you have a choice of providing exercise pens or bunny proofing your house.

Even the smallest apartment can offer enough safe running time and space for one or two rabbits. If your house or apartment is small, and you adopt multiple animals, you may have to exercise them in shifts. No bunny will feel energetic all day long, but bunnies, nonetheless, need enough free-running time to ensure the opportunity to move about.

MINIMUM SPACE REQUIREMENTS

The following options allow bunnies adequate "time out" within the limitations of a small house.

Option 1: *Separated rest and run areas.*
Run time is at least 4 hrs daily or 30 hrs weekly

Number of Rabbits	Rest Area (sq ft)	Rest Area Dimensions	Run Area (sq. ft.)	Run Dimensions
1-2	8	2x4 ft.	24	3x8 or 4x6 ft.
3-4	16	4x4 ft.	24	3x8 or 4x6 ft.
5-6	24	3x8 or 4x6 ft.	48	6x8 ft.

Option 2: *Combined rest and run areas.*
Run time is 24 hrs daily

Number of Rabbits	Run/Rest Area (sq. ft.)	Run/Rest Dimensions
1-4	24 ft.	3x8 or 4x6 ft.
5-6	48 ft.	6x8 ft.

COMMENT ON OPTION 2: *If your bunnies make cleanup difficult (e.g., grab the broom and jump into the litterbox just as you try to change the litter), you can put them in carriers until your chores are done.*

Option 3: *Combined rest and run areas in a bunnyproofed house.* Run time is 24 hrs daily.

The above tables show how much run time is needed in what size area. Living and running areas can be combined in a large space. The next chapter will cover where and how to set up those spaces. ∎

PHOTO: CAROLYN LONG

Setting Up Space

Your lifestyle will determine your choice in meeting your bunny's needs—from a large cage or condo to a bunny-proofed room to an entire bunny-proofed house.

Left: Emerson and Eddie's home in the study
Inset: Jennifer Grimes and Emerson

Habitat Setup

Assuming that your bunny will be confined at times (especially in new residency), that confinement should be close to where you spend time, e.g., your bedroom or your work area, so that you can have some interaction and conversation. The bunny areas should also have plenty of natural light (not direct sunlight without a shady option). Temperature between 60°-75° is comfortable for a rabbit, but more cold than heat can be tolerated.

In addition to bunny's comfort, her living space must allow access by the caregiver. You have a choice between two basic types of habitats—*reach* inside and *step* inside. Within those, additional options are available.

REACH -INSIDE HABITATS

Whether it's a single-level cage or a two-story condo, the back corners have to be within your arm's reach. This limits the depth to about 2 1/2 feet, but not the length (the longer the better). The overall cage size should be influenced by the amount of time spent inside it, as well as the size of the rabbit. Generally, the space should be 3-4 times the (stretched out) adult body-length. Remember this if you now have a baby in a starter cage. Two-story condos, connected by a ramp or a step-up can add living space within the same footprint. All cages and condos, however, should be thought of only as bunny bedrooms, not as their entire play space.

The cage or condo should have large side-opening doors, and if it includes a top door, be certain that the top door clamps securely on all sides, so that it can't be pushed up from inside the cage, (posing danger of strangulation). The small-animal cages sold in many pet stores are not adequate for rabbits to live in but might be occasionally useful for transportation or for temporary sick beds.

My own feelings about cages have gone through many transitions over the past 20 years. At one time I decided to get rid of my cages altogether. Fortunately, they only made it to the garage, when I realized that it would be very difficult to treat a sick bunny without one. How would I confine a bunny with a back injury? or keep a hypothermic bunny warm? I brought my best cage back into the house and set it up in a corner, where it can be used quickly during an emergency.

One of the best changes in rabbit care in the past few years has been the explosion of new ideas in rabbit housing. As rabbit people share ideas on the Internet, rabbits benefit with wonderful environments. If you are not into constructing your own cage or condo, pet-supply stores now carry a good variety, or you can order one online.

Open door policy *converts a store-bought cage to a hospitality room for friends.*

PHOTO: AMY ESPIE

STEP-INSIDE HABITATS

The concept of "large enough for a human to sit in" came from Carolyn Long of Milwaukee, as she described the large habitat she had built for her rabbits. My first thought was, Why would you want to sit in your rabbit's cage? After spending many hours sitting inside my rabbits' pens while grooming and visiting, I don't ask that question anymore.

Xpens: The versatility of puppy pens, often called exercise pens or xpens, make them a popular choice for housing rabbits indoors. They are available in nearly any pet supply store. They can be expanded by adding sections and can be arranged in a variety of shapes. An alternative is a plastic "play yard" for (human) toddlers, available in department/variety stores. Metal pens are more robust, however, since they can't be chewed.

The pen folds down and can be moved about. (Temporary height extenders may need to be clamped on, if the new bunny is a jumper or climber). It's a good investment even if you plan to bunny-proof and allow your bun free run of the house. You may pull it out of storage when you get a second rabbit or when you bunny-sit for a friend.

You can protect your carpeting from hay and other debris by setting the pen on top of a patch of linoleum or a chair mat. Or you can install the pen on a raised platform. A durable floor surface that we are currently using is FRP (fiberglass-reinforced plastic) glued onto plywood. The slightly bumpy

Xpens (above) can be set up in a rectangle on a patch of linoleum, rolled out over carpeting.
Wire shelving (left) is assembled on FRP-covered platforms that are edged with wooden retaining strips.

surface (enough for traction) is highly cleanable, virtually chew proof, and is available at most home-improvement stores.

Wire shelving: Rabbit people are also using wire shelving creatively for bunny housing. This can be done with 15x48-inch wire shelf panels or 14-inch squares that clip together in modules. I find these are lots of fun to build (like Tinkertoys). I like the flexibility of being able to reshape the living spaces, building them up or out, to fit the number and nature of the bunnies who live here. Use pliers and a small hammer to tap the panels apart and squeeze them back together as needed. Cover upper decks with a rug or board to prevent feet from slipping through wide-mesh wire.

"Socializing can be a pre-bedtime or wakeup ritual."

DOUBLE-DUTY ROOMS

Sharing a room with your bunny is fun. You can be inventive. Could you set up some bunny space at one end of your kitchen away from the heat of the stove? Or maybe your dining room works better. In Carolyn Long's well used dining room, one chair provides a step to a bunny salad-bar. And dinner guests, seated at the table, may be nudged into petting the bunny under their chair.

A breakfast nook, a service porch, or any room off a room can be made into bunny space, with

Breakfast nook with a baby gate (right) *converts easily to a bunny room that doubles as a human sitting room.*
Comfort corner *A wicker tunnel provides the front entrance to a cardboard warren where Emerson (unseen) is rearranging the bedding. Eddie stands guard from a fake-fleece rug (extras on the roof).*

regular human activity nearby. Do you have a study or a home office? This can be ideal. Check out Jennifer Grimes and Brian Carter's study on page 21. Your projects may be inspired when you share workspace.

Everybody has to sleep. If bunnies hang out in your bedroom, you will automatically have time together. Socializing can be a pre-bedtime or wakeup ritual. Take some extra time to wind down at night or have your coffee in bed in the morning.

A DEDICATED ROOM

If you have a whole room you can spare in your house, it might be converted to bunny's living and play space. This arrangement works best when there are several rabbits or groups of rabbits for companionship.

Since human interaction is not built in to a dedicated spare room, visit your bunny often throughout the day and spend a lot of time petting, grooming and simply sitting.

Another way to minimize isolation in a spare room is to use a see-through baby gate instead of a solid door.

THE ENTIRE HOUSE

The last option of course requires extensive bunny-proofing everywhere. In this plan, all rooms are double-duty rooms, shared by you and your bunny. Even so, you will most likely find that your bunny has favorite spots. ∎

Furnishing the Living Area

ANY SIZE LIVING AREA MUST HAVE fundamental furnishings for eating, sleeping and tending to toilet needs. The area should also include a few recreational and chewable items. The basic list consists of the following:

Water crock. Purchase crocks or heavy clay bowls only from reputable pet-product suppliers. Decorator or designer pottery from other sources may contain lead.

Hanging water bottles with sipper tubes take up less space than crocks and make better use of smaller areas but require an attachable surface (cage wall or fencing). Keep the water out of direct sunlight (which encourages the growth of algae).

Chow bowl. Where space is not a problem, bowls can be used for food and as well as water. Heavy clay is preferable to lightweight plastic. Plastic bowls should have an extra-wide lip that can't be gripped in bunny's teeth and turned over.

Hanging feeders, like water bottles, allow more floor space inside a small area. Bear in mind that unlimited feed, as dispensed in a feeder, can eventually result in an overfed obese rabbit.

Litterbox(es). Various sizes and shapes are available to fit your bunny's space. Some even have a lowered entrance for special needs.

Washable rug. If your bunny has to run on hard surfaces, give his feet a rest with padded areas. Soft rugs of fake fleece are ideal, as well as felt-type indoor/outdoor carpeting, cut to machine-washable sizes.

Baby blankets are preferable to terry cloth towels. If you use any fabric that begins to ravel, cut off strings immediately or transfer it to your "cleaning rags."

Hay container. Whether this is a shallow box or deep tub or a hanging basket, your bunny needs hay, and you need a place to put it

Small toys. These are more of a necessity than you might think. A generous supply of chew toys and nudge/toss toys (see next chapter) should be supplied in every living space.

Large toys. If the living space and running space are combined, then exercise equipment (see page 28) should also be included in the living area. ∎

Basic necessities: A water bottle hangs as an option on the wire mesh panel. Clay dishes sit on top of a fake fleece rug along with plastic toys and a partially chewed square of seagrass mat. A plastic tub serves as a litterbox, with a hay hanger attached at one end. Nicholas and Leslie also have a daytime pen outdoors (page 27), with their cardboard and a hay/straw box supplied there.

Running Space

Square Room and Long Hall: *Roselyn peruses the long hall at the HRS Rabbit Center (above) then runs its length. Trixie hops about in a square room (left) to wherever her interests take her.*

The running area might be included in the living space if the space is large enough (indicated on page 20) to provide adequate exercise. Or you can set up a large pen within a room or fence off a section of a room in the shape that pleases your bunny.

If you absolutely have no space indoors, a covered outdoor playpen might serve for daytime exercise. For this you might use an enclosed porch or balcony, where at least one wall is part of your house. However, do not leave a rabbit unattended on a porch with public access. "Enclosed" means full fencing on all sides and overhead, even at upper-story levels. The fact is that predatory birds can and do snatch rabbits from balconies.

I no longer recommend the use of a harness and leash in public places, even though you are on hand to swoop up your bunny if a dog approaches. You may not be sure of the chemicals or contamination that might be present on the ground in a public area. If you insist on taking your bunny on an outing, a portable playpen is a safer choice.

STATIONARY OUTDOOR RUNS

The pen size we use for our bunnies' daytime exercise is 3 x 8 feet, which gives them enough room to kick up their heels. One-inch welded wire covers all

EXERCISE OR STRETCH-OUT SPACE is beyond the basic eating and resting area. Adequate space is assumed when bunny has the run of the entire house, but running space can also be provided in one or two rooms. The type of activity performed is influenced by the shape of the area—long, wide, high, low. For some reason a long hall seems to entice bunnies to run the distance, whereas a square room induces dashing in short spurts.

PHOTOS: TOP, MARINELL HARRIMAN; INSET, AMY ESPIE

"Because the number of predators increases significantly at dusk, always bring your bunny in at night."

four sides and the bottom of a wooden frame. When we had a large backyard and could turn the runs over to clean them, we covered the floors with a thick layer of straw.

When we moved into a house with a tiny backyard, we no longer had that option. Our runs had to become stationary. Using the old frame (3x8) with 1-inch wire mesh still in place, we set up three sections within each run. One end is covered with bricks. The middle section is furnished with a washable rug, and the far end has a brick-rimmed hay area over the wire mesh floor.

A smaller area of straw is easier to replace (without completely filling our recycle barrel), but the main advantage is that the bunnies have choices. On hot days they can stretch out on the cool bricks. When the weather is chilly they can snuggle on the rug, and they always have access to straw or hay.

Wire tops allow ventilation on warm days, but we add solid (plywood or corrugated plastic) covers when the weather is cold and damp.

These are daytime playgrounds only. Because the number of predators increases significantly at dusk, *always* bring your bunny in at night.   ∎

Plan view: (above) shows the hinged top, which allows humans to reach utensils and equipment or to climb inside to visit the bunnies.
Elevation view: (right) takes a look through the bunnies' side door into the varied brick, rug, and hay areas.

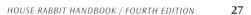

Gymnasium Equipment

URNISHING EXERCISE SPACE differs from furnishing living space in that toys included here are to engage large-muscle activity, such as stretching, climbing, running, leaping (rather than just chewing exercises). A few store-bought items with simple home conversions can satisfy just about any need your bunny may have for leap-over, climb-onto, run-through, dig-out, or dive-into equipment.

Tunnels: Cardboard tubes, which make ideal rabbit tunnels, are actually concrete forms sold in building supply stores. Or you can try a carpeted cat tunnel from your pet supply store. A great combination is a long hall to run, with tunnels to shoot through. If you can't get a tunnel, you can line up a row of cardboard boxes with holes cut in the sides.

Baskets are considered chew toys, but in a stack, they may stimulate some climbing action. Cardboard boxes can also be stacked creatively into a climbing arrangement. Use your imagination to design your bunny's gymnasium.

Exercise Projects. Bunnies are natural workers, who enjoy a project. It might be digging all the newspapers out of a tub, or rearranging the blankets on your bed. Toss some old rugs up there for them to work on. Another variation of this project is to stuff a bunch of newspapers into a cardboard tube or behind your couch,

Mountains to climb: *(upper left)* A rug covered ramp up a sawhorse and a stack of wicker baskets *(upper right)* induce some climbing action. *Tireless tube:* Jeffrey *(below)* circles back for repeated runs through his tunnel in the Rabbit Center hallway.

or put a phone directory in a flat box, and watch the energy exerted by your bunny in digging them out.

Hay tubs. These are more than litterboxes topped with hay, so they need to be deep enough to dive into and dig around. The exercise is not in eating hay but jumping in and out of a deep tub.

Ramps. Daily exercise can be largely in getting to where they want to go—as a means to an end. Ramps can be used just about anywhere. I've seen them used to make bunnies climb to get to a favorite place on a dresser or to a lookout perch by a window.

Wheel carts give mobility to disabled bunnies, allowing them sone exercise, too. With all the equipment available, there's something for everybody. ■

PHOTOS: UPPER, CAROLYN LONG; LOWER, MARINELL HARRIMAN,

Bunny-Proofing Your Home

We should not want our rabbits to entirely lose their natural urges to chew, dig, explore, and claim territory. We can simply provide outlets for these needs.

Left: *Emy sits in her chewable house.*
Inset: *Bill Cole of Ohio and rabbit Dudley.*

PHOTOS: ABOVE, MARINELL HARRIMAN; INSET, KRISTI COLE

Hiding Temptations

BEFORE ALLOWING YOUR BUNNY the full run of the house, survey the accessible areas. Her first running time should be carefully supervised. Have you moved all valuable books, magazines, and potted plants to higher shelves? Are all electrical cords covered up or out of reach? If you don't want bunny to chomp down on your computer cords, don't allow the cords to dangle in her chewing range. Rabbits cannot resist nibbling on these long "vines." Is that chair pushed all the way under the desk when left unoccupied? Otherwise it can be used as a springboard by a whiskered explorer to access the desktop.

Your bunny-proofing efforts may require no more than picking up a few items. On the other hand, additional chewing temptations may be waiting to be discovered. Chances are you won't know how well your home is bunny-proofed until bunny has tested your handiwork.

COVER-UPS

Any of those things that hide or enclose the forbidden article, such as the phone cord, we call a

PHOTO: AMY ESPIE

Useful cover-ups: As Oliver explores the world, his humans protect the ports with throws and metal fencing (right). Daphne, intrigued with the wicker hamper, has forgotten what's behind it (left).

cover-up. Numerous items would adequately serve this purpose, but you will want to use those that will not destroy your home decor at the same time. Some of the following have worked for us without being too obtrusive:

Chair mats can be purchased at office-supply stores in a variety of sizes. They cover problem areas of linoleum, hardwood flooring, or carpeting.

Seagrass rugs serve the same purpose as chair mats but are intended to be chewed up and replaced.

Wooden bumpers are thin strips of untreated wood, tacked onto a baseboard to protect the baseboard and serve as a chew block.

Plexiglas in 24-inch sheets can protect wall areas above baseboards without severely interfering with decor.

Vinyl tubing is sold by the foot in hardware stores and it comes in a variety of diameters. With a sharp utility knife, cut the tube lengthwise and push the electrical cord inside.

Furniture arrangement. This is also a way to hide wiring. Block the access to the electrical outlets with a piece of furniture.

Blanket throws can protect against toenails and teeth when tossed across upholstery or beds.

REPELLENTS

If your bunny really has a mindset to chew on forbidden items, you may extend your repertoire of repellents, cover-ups, or diversions. Repellents are any of those odors that bunny finds repulsive. Some of these articles you may already have on your dresser (perfumes, shaving lotions, or other fragrances), and others you have in your garage but not in your house (carburetor cleaner, motor oil). Rejected men sometimes believe that their rabbits show gender preference. Don't take it personally. Rabbits are not fond of men *or* women who have recently made automotive repairs.

Dog and cat repellents can be used, but don't over do it! Dense atomizing will keep bunny, and you too, completely away from the area. A tiny spray is enough. Repellents should be reapplied daily until bunny has lost interest in the forbidden object.

Many people have experimented with tastes, applying bitters or red-pepper sauce. I find these inconsistent for keeping bunnies out of trouble. Turning them off with bad odors before they chomp down is safer. ∎

PHOTOS: UPPER RIGHT, JIM STONEBURNER; LOWER LEFT, AMY ESPIE

Diversions via Toys

RABBITS ARE PROGRAMMED both mentally and physiologically to chew. Their bodies require it for nutritional and functional reasons. These needs are manifested in recreational chewing. Rabbits need indigestible organic fiber—but not synthetic fiber, such as your carpet. Give your rabbits such engaging things to chew that they don't even think about chewing the carpet.

At the top of the list in bunny chewables are straw and wood of all kinds. Straw can be given in a bale, in a bag, loose in a box, or woven into baskets or rugs.

Toys in action: Brit (below) prefers twigs and slinkies. Duststorm (right) chooses a chewable wooden block. Daphne (below) tosses a wire ball.

Loose straw can be messy, but confined in a large tub, it can provide an abundance of chewing pleasure without getting all over your carpet.

Disposable straw and wicker baskets come in many sizes and shapes. Bunnies love them all. Busy Bunny Baskets™, filled with edibles, are available online and in many pet-supply shops. Also, untreated wood blocks or dried firewood with bark, as well as small dried tree-branches are good for chewing. Check the toxic list on page 61.

In addition to chewables, rabbits like toss, roll, scoot, and dig-about toys. They are known to be quite imaginative with some of them. They espe-

PHOTOS: LEFT, CAROLYN LONG; TOP, RIGHT, MARINELL HARRIMAN

cially enjoy noisy toys at 3:00 a.m.— jingly, rattly, bouncy things, such as mason-jar lids, batta-bouts, car keys, empty soup cans, and baby toys (make sure they are only hard-plastic, non-breakable).

Getting inside: *Phoebe lurks in a paper bag (upper left). Ninja investigates a cup. (upper right) Oliver in a basket, almost (lower left). Nim exercises her teeth on cardboard instead of her human's house (lower right).*

On the quieter side are large rubber balls or nudge-and-roll cylinders, such as empty salt cartons, toilet paper spools, and paper towel spools. A towel on a slick floor provides something for bunny to scoot around, bunch up, spread out, pat down, then roll up and scoot around again.

Cardboard has multiple uses. Rabbits can find all kinds of things to do with a cardboard box. They can sit inside it, hop on top, chew it, scratch it, dig in it, and knock it about. Paper bags serve similar purposes, except for hop-onto platforms.

All kinds of toys are good for you. They save your house while they save your bunny's inventive mind from boredom. ■

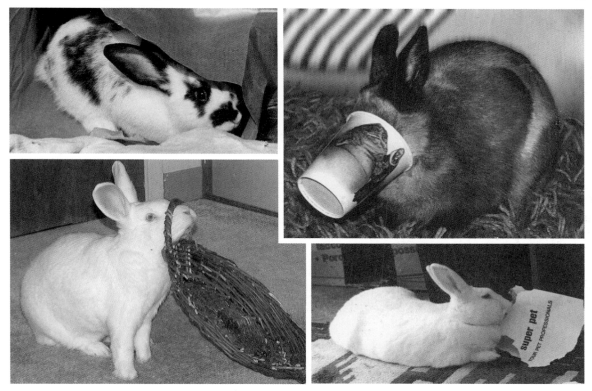

PHOTOS: UPPER, TANIA HARRIMAN, MARINELL HARRIMAN; LOWER: JIM STONEBURNER, AMY ESPIE

Safety Checklist

BUNNY-PROOFING is assumed to mean that it is done to protect your furnishings, floors, and walls. A more important reason to bunny-proof is to save your bunny. So much of what you have in your house is toxic if chewed.

Have you thought of bunny-proofing your yard as well? From harmful plants and parasites?

INDOOR SAFETY

In addition to the cover-ups you have already installed, be sure to check other items of potential danger when you leave the house. Much of this you do anyway, but include a burrower or climber in the mix and then estimate the potential.

You may have others to add, specific to your house, but if you keep a list by your front door, it's easy to check it off when you go out, and you will have a much better time, with the peace of mind in knowing that your bunny is safe.

❏ Electrical appliances turned off?
❏ Heat/cooling vents covered securely with tightly attached face plates?
❏ Windows closed?
❏ Outside doors closed?
❏ Doors to any incompatible animals secured?
❏ Step-ups removed from dangerously high places?
❏ Tight places blocked off (behind refrigerator or stove)?
❏ If your bunny is caged, are spring latches completely secure (or replaced with bolting latches)?
❏ Toilet lid closed?
❏ If your bunny is a jumper or a climber, have you extended the height of the fencing/baby-gate?

OUTDOOR SAFETY

A completely safe outdoor hutch seldom exists. Even when elevated several feet off the ground, wire cages do not prevent the possibility of self-induced trauma due to fright when predators are near.

A little known fact is that a predator can kill a rabbit without physical contact. All it may take is the presence of the predator—within distance to be seen, smelled, or heard. Whether thrashing in a hutch or fleeing across the yard in panic, the rabbit may incur permanent injury or enter a state of shock that results in death.

Predatory animals in urban areas include dogs, feral cats, large birds, and raccoons (the most commonly underestimated threats to rabbits). Raccoons come up through storm drains into very urban areas and find prey at night. Farther out in more rural areas, the list widens to include coyotes, foxes, wolves, large reptiles, and sometimes mountain lions.

Running loose outside, a rabbit is all the more likely to be exposed to predators, as well as the danger from toxic plants, pesticides, parasites, soil contamination, or moving vehicles.

Ensuring outdoor safety includes these conditions:
1. Yard is enclosed on all sides by a secure fence at least 6 feet high.
2. Yard has been cleared of toxic plants (page 61).
3. Bunnies occupy outdoor area only during daytime hours.
4. A responsible adult is within seeing and hearing distance to bunnies playing outdoors.

Bunnies should be brought inside at dusk, and under no circumstances should a bunny run loose in your yard in your absence. If you plan on being away for a few hours during Bunny's time out, use securely covered playpens or runs.

Lastly, if you have stationary runs in your yard, be sure that they are closed even when your bunnies are not in them. This is to minimize exposure to parasitic diseases that can be spread by the urine and feces of feral animals (see page 69). If you store your hay outside, keep it covered and inaccessible to other animals, especially raccoons. ■

Litterbox Training

Replace rules with provisions. Set out too many rather than too few litterboxes and make then so inviting that Bunny cannot resist getting into them.

Left: *Jeffrey occupies his litterbox.*
Inset: *Karen Winstead of Ohio with bunny Zoe.*

PHOTOS: ABOVE, BOB HARRIMAN; INSET, PENNY ADAMS

Location and Method

RABBITS OF ANY AGE train themselves through their own course of habit. Your job is to direct the habit into a mutually agreeable location. The litterbox should be wonderfully inviting, never to be associated with punishment. Reprimands have no place in bunny training and, in fact, greatly interfere in establishing natural good habits.

Place the litterbox in a convenient location so that it's easy for a bunny to do the "right" thing. In my house, bunnies show preference to places rather than materials. I can switch litters or switch litterboxes, no matter. But if I move the litterbox to another location, they often use the prior location with or without a litterbox. One time I lined their boxes with newspaper, forgetting to put litter on top. A few hours later, I noticed all the rabbits had used the newspaper alone, without waiting for the addition of litter material.

For all needs: Litterboxes come in many sizes, shapes and styles. Michelle uses a converted carrier with a low entry for easy access.

For some bunnies, litter material is most important. For others (like mine), it's strictly the location, no matter what type of litter is used.

When I trained my first bunny many years ago, I didn't even know I was training her. I spread newspapers all over my kitchen in anticipation of the mess I thought I was going to have. In the next few days, I noticed that I was only picking up two newspapers. Then I was down to one. I thought, Hmm. What if I slid a litterbox under that newspaper?

BEGINNER TIME

Bunny's first few weeks in your home should be spent primarily in a small bunny-proofed area described in the previous chapter. Start with a litterbox

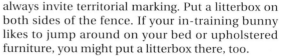

"If your bunny is not becoming self-trained, you may be giving too much space too soon."

in Bunny's preferred corner. Rabbits start using a litterbox because they like it. Well-placed hay hangers and toys encourage them to linger a bit and even take care of some personal grooming.

When you expand bunny's starter space to include more territory, add more litterboxes. Again, it's better to start with too many rather than too few litterboxes. This is not forever. Eventually, a favorite location will emerge.

MARKING TERRITORY

Rabbits need to mark new territory with urine or feces in order to feel that they belong in that environment (more noticeable when there are multiple animals). If the environment has plenty of litterboxes that they can dutifully "mark," then everybody will be happy. The space on both sides of a see-through fence between competitive rabbits will

Training area: An indoor play yard (below) can be set up anywhere in the house. This small area is still large enough to include a litterbox and a seagrass mat.
A temporary litterbox (right) can be placed anywhere, even on a chair during training.

always invite territorial marking. Put a litterbox on both sides of the fence. If your in-training bunny likes to jump around on your bed or upholstered furniture, you might put a litterbox there, too.

Exuberant bunnies often like to mark any new play area immediately upon entrance. If you take them straight to a litterbox in the new area, they soon get the idea that the litterbox is the territory to mark, and they associate it with additional freedom. Within a few weeks, they'll make a beeline for the litterbox on their own.

NATURAL ROUTINES

As Bunny matures and carves out his territory, his regular use of litterboxes should be a natural evolution of what he wants to do anyway. If your bunny is not becoming self-trained, you may be giving too much space too soon. Or you may not be making the litterbox(es) enticing enough. Keep working on making them irresistible.

Good toilet habits may take several weeks or months to achieve, depending on maturity. Don't expect a perfectly house-trained bunny at 6 weeks old. Post-adolescent spayed or neutered rabbits are much more reliably housetrained. Adolescent rabbits are hormone driven and often lose good litterbox routines until after their neuter surgery.

Older spayed or neutered rabbits are generally easier to train because they're more inclined to settle into a routine. Healthy older rabbits have often disproved the notion that a rabbit must be young to be trainable. Rabbit routines that do not include some degree of good toilet habits may be indicative of a health problem. ∎

PHOTOS: LEFT, MARINELL HARRIMAN; RIGHT, AMIE ESPIE

Litter Materials

SAFE(ER) LITTERS FOR RABBITS have become much more available in the past few years, and nearly all pet-supply stores carry at least one of them. Safe litters are made from relatively benign materials such as paper fiber, mountain grasses, wheat, corn cob, and specially processed woods (with re-

Invitation with hay: *There are two ways to use hay as litterbox enticement. Fill or top off a deep litterbox or tub (upper), or hang the hay over the litterbox (lower). Both ways keep the hay contained.*

duced phenols). Avoid aromatic softwood shavings, such as pine or cedar, as well as clumping litters and dusty clays. Of course you don't want bunny to chew and swallow large amounts of any kind of litter. If you've purchased one that your bunny finds too tasty, then switch to another. Litters can cause internal damage and should not be ingested.

Topping the litter with hay or straw is preferable to allowing bunny to eat litter, however, the litterboxes will need to be changed frequently, to avoid mold or bacterial growth.

Hay can be composted, but when used as litter in large quantities, the extra bulk may present a disposal problem for apartment dwellers. A tidier plan might be to hook a hay hanger over a newspaper-lined or litter-filled box. A hanger can be placed anywhere, but over the litterbox is especially useful for catching falling debris.

FROM MAILBOX TO LITTERBOX

Alternative litters are also available in your home or office mailbox. Legal advisors tell you to shred all your sensitive information such as credit card offers. I was doing my own shredding until I realized that I have built in shredders and junk-mail terminators right in my bedroom. It would certainly challenge the would-be identity thief to rummage through the soggy mutilated remains of our junk mail once it has been processed through our bunnies' litterboxes.

At one time I would not have considered using rugs or fabric in a litterbox. I thought it would cause confusion when running on the carpet. Not so. Again, in my house it's the place rather than the material that is important to the bunny. As to cleanup, it's a matter of preference. Is it cheaper/easier/more environmentally friendly to run an additional washer load in your area, or do you have a good disposal/recycling service? ∎

Bonding Buddies

Companions enhance your rabbit's life, without diminishing affection for you. Rabbits live naturally in groups and are capable of multiple friendships.

Left: Wanda dog, Tess and Tania cats, and Nim rabbit share a rug.
Inset: Jon, Cece, and Abby join noses.

PHOTOS: ABOVE, AMY ESPIE; INSET, BRANDON CHEE

Rabbits with Cats

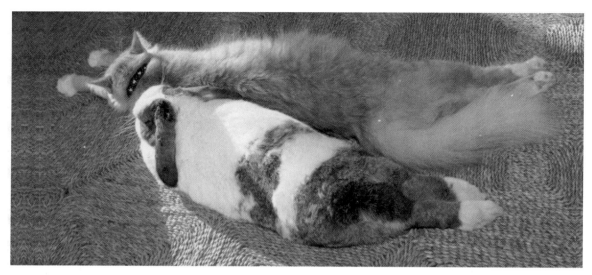

As much as we encourage companionship for all rabbits, this is not always with each other. In some situations, the demands of their own society can be too stressful for certain individuals to live happily. These animals often relate better to companions of another species. This may be the case with individuals of many species. I've had cats who detest each other but adore the rabbits. The reverse can also be true.

Cats and rabbits in the same household can be very compatible. Many people who adopt rabbits already have cats. Cats and rabbits do not need to bed down together (although many of them do) in order to have an interesting and reciprocal relationship. Our first rabbit, Herman, and our cat, Nice, never touched, but they interacted in chase games—in and out of paper bags. A game of retaliation occurred daily between the two. After being ambushed from behind the door, Herman waited until nap time to throw herself on top of the peacefully dozing cat.

Phoebe, Herman's successor, developed intimate rapport with Octavia. This was the kind of relationship that meant when Phoebe was sick and needed around-the-clock care, Octavia stayed by her side for a full 48 hours—until the crisis passed. (We believe that Octavia saved Phoebe's life.) Friendship is governed by individuals.

A LITTLE PRECAUTION

Introductions during feisty adolescence of either species should be more carefully supervised. A lively, boisterous teenage cat can put dangerous claws into an unsuspecting bunny. And, of course, you should avoid giving a very young bunny (rat size) to a full-grown cat. On the other hand, big rabbits can bully a lighter weight cat, so equal size usually makes a better match. And cats of all ages should have their nails trimmed very short. Neither species should ever be declawed.   ■

PHOTOS: BOTH PAGES, AMY ESPIE

Rabbits with Guinea Pigs

RABBITS AND GUINEA PIGS usually fall into fairly easy friendships. Many rabbit rescuers have picked up guinea pigs among the rescues. I have.

How could I go to an animal shelter and remove the two rabbits and leave that one small kennel mate behind? I have to say that clinically speaking, rabbits and guinea pigs are not supposed to be housed together. Practically speaking, we (rabbit rescuers) do it anyway. The danger is that some bacteria that are harmless in one species may cause trouble in another. For this reason, guinea-pig books advise against caging colonies of rabbits and guinea pigs together.

Sharing chew toys:
Branches are suitable for both guinea pigs and rabbits.

Again, our practical experience shows mixed species happily sharing environments and living long lives. If you are putting together household companions and live in reasonable cleanliness, the risk appears to be minimal. If you are going into an animal-production business, you will need to get a different book.

SHARED PLAYGROUNDS

Many people enjoy building guinea pigs elaborate habitats as they do for their rabbits. Sometimes a fenced-in playground is provided that the pigs and bunnies can share. The fence or wall can be as low as one foot high if you want your rabbits, but not your guinea pigs, to have access to the rest of the house.

If you let your guinea pigs have part-time run of the house, you need to put a lot of little flat trays along the edges of the room. Another place they may designate as a bathroom is under the bed. We discovered this one time as we we pulled out a flat storage box and found it had been converted to a guinea-pig litterbox.

Guinea pigs can eat high-quality rabbit pellets, but they have additional vitamin C requirements. Supplements of bell peppers, tomatoes, and oranges won't harm your rabbit, so they can share treats. Rabbits and guinea pigs also have similar sensitivities to certain antibiotics.

The veterinarian who sees your rabbit will be familiar with guinea pigs. If you choose a guinea-pig companion for your rabbit, you should familiarize yourself with the special needs of that species. Have your veterinarian recommend reading material. ■

Rabbits with Dogs

ONE MAJOR CHANGE since 1985's first edition of *House Rabbit Handbook* is that it's now well known that with careful observation and supervision bunnies can get along with well-behaved dogs, cats, and others in a "mixed" environment. More caution is required, however, for introducing rabbits to dogs safely. Since the success of the introduction depends on the behavior of the dog, it's absolutely crucial that the dog not chase if the rabbit runs. She should know "down-stay," "good dog," "gentle," and "off" before an introduction is attempted.

INITIAL BEDLAM

When we brought 8-month-old Xena in the door, all the rabbits in our house started thumping in frenzy. Teddy and Lilac scurried out of the living room, and our cat, Octavia, bowed up her back and hissed and growled. The first evening looked like nothing was going to work. The very scent of a dog in the house, even in a distant room, made all the rabbits very uneasy. The first task was just to get them accustomed to her presence in the house. Even today, whenever we bring new rabbits in from the shelter, we have to give them plenty of time to adjust to the presence of a dog in the house.

We started with a 4 x 4-foot puppy pen to provide Xena with a place where she could be observed as unthreatening by the rabbits. We set up the pen with food and water dishes, bed, and toys, but instead of a litterbox, of course, we took her out on harness and leash several times a day. The cat began to sit on the coffee table next to Xena, where she watched with curiosity. We managed the next few weeks in the following stages:

1. Rotated use of the yard. Xena used the backyard before the rabbits went out in the morning and after they came in at night. (We walked her on leash at other times.)

2. A puppy pen part of the day. Curious rabbits could observe Xena, who was contained in the pen. Free-running rabbits could be observed by the dog in a non-chase environment.

3. Supervised (leashed) time outside the pen.

4. Unleashed time outside the pen when the rabbits

PHOTO: AMY ESPIE

> "... Amy Espie had advised us to avoid situations that require reprimand—
> so that the rabbits are not a source of frustration."

were in their cages. The rabbits gradually became accustomed to the noises and strange movements of the dog . They could sniff noses and get acquainted through the safety of the wire mesh.

5. *Dog-style exercise* (with us)—running, jumping, fetching a ball, to expend her energy.

6. *Participation in duties.* Xena began to make the rounds with us as we gave nightly feedings. Her first real introduction was to a crippled rabbit who lived on our service porch. As I talked gently to Rousseau, filled his dish, and stroked him, Xena mimicked my manner with gentle grooming.

7. *Co-mingling in our presence.* We took down the puppy pen and allowed Xena freedom of the house. Not wanting to risk a sudden overwhelming impulse of a young playful pup, we never left her alone with the rabbits during the first year.

As she spent more and more time freely co-mingling with rabbits in our presence, we began to leave them together for short periods during their quiet times of day.

8. *Reward without reprimand.* Xena's experience with the rabbits has always been positive. Dog trainer Amy Espie had advises us to avoid situations that require reprimand—so that the rabbits are not a source of frustration. This is a fundamental that Amy defined years ago for training any animal living in a human environment. It's called "setting up for success."

After a total of six unhurried months, we were

Wanda meets the boys: *Amy Espie's pitbull (above) is anything but "vicious," after weeks of very careful socializing and training.*
Bunny meets dog *(right): Donna Jensen introduces her rabbit Sawyer to her gentle dog, Teddy.*

rewarded with free running rabbits living comfortably with a young dog, who no longer required supervision and could be left alone with the rabbits for an indeterminate period of time.

The above scenario is fairly typical. The sidebar on the next two pages follows the progress of an extremely challenging dog. Additional rabbit-dog articles are available online at www.rabbit.org. ∎

PHOTOS: TOP, AMY ESPIE; INSET, WALTER JENSEN

A Kinder, Gentler Baran

BY BILL HARRIMAN

How does one manage safe cohabitation with a dog who has aggressive tendencies? We had to confront this issue when we brought home Baran, a Lab-Pit mix, from our local shelter. Animal Care and Control officers found him tied at the side of a freeway. We figure that he was probably bred to be a fighting dog but for some reason his original "caretaker" lost interest. As a 6-8 month old, he was friendly but a little skittish. However, as he matured, he began to reveal a territorial and protective nature that made us think twice about introducing him to new people or new dogs, although he remains terrific with our family and people he knows. He is also well behaved with his companion Peppy, an elderly dog with a slight handicap.

We have a fairly large and rustic backyard with tall oat grass that provides a bunny paradise, but we initially didn't even think of letting Sonic, Knuckles, and Tails run in the same yard as our dogs, since Baran pretty much goes after anything that moves: squirrels, raccoons, whatever. It did seem a shame, though, not to let the bunnies romp when the weather was good. We decided that we'd try to figure out a solution.

We started by building a run in the backyard that was secure from the dogs but still allowed them to see and sniff the bunnies. The initial introduction produced a predictable result: Baran got very excited and started to chase around the perimeter of the run, with Peppy following his lead. The bunnies became anxious and began to dart about, exacerbating the situation. We strongly reprimanded Baran and eventually calmed him, and everything started to settle down. We repeated this daily for about a week until the novelty wore off. The dogs would still walk over to a bunny from time to time and sniff, but in a very low-key way. Knowing that strong corrections require a foundation of positive reinforcement, we made sure to respond to these nonaggressive non-encounters with plenty of praise. Occasionally there would be a scuffle between Sonic and Knuckles in the run, which would induce Baran to hurry over and bark. Even this kind of activity became commonplace after a while, and Baran would investigate casually, then wander off. We praised him lavishly for this calm behavior.

We eventually built up the courage to try Baran out with the bunnies loose in the yard, although Baran was far from loose: knowing that tragic accidents can happen in an instant, we kept him right next to us with not only a short leash but also a muzzle. Perhaps the muzzle wasn't necessary, but we weren't taking any chances with Baran's powerful jaws and quick responses. We left Peppy indoors initially because we didn't want to set the scene for a hunting mentality, which is what happens when an unfortunate wild animal meanders into the yard.

With one of us holding Baran tightly, the other placed first Sonic, then Knuckles, then Tails down in succession about two feet in front of him. Our thinking here was that we wanted to establish that the bunnies were placed in the yard on purpose by us, and were thereby "authorized" to be there.

As expected, Baran lunged toward them but we sternly pulled him back and scolded him. The bunnies were at first shocked at their new freedom, and didn't move around very much, but after a while they began to scamper about. Baran was

Sonic gets authorized as the author's sons Nico (above), Aladdin and Rian pitch in to help Baran understand the backyard rules of engagement

PHOTOS: BOTH PAGES, BILL HARRIMAN

> "...This is by no means a daily activity, but a special outdoor time that we do when we have time to supervise."

absolutely beside himself, and started to whine and lunge. Each time he did so, we quickly followed with a correction. He became so conditioned over the course of 3 or 4 half-hour "sessions" that he started to modify his behavior on his own, without correction from us. We responded to this positive behavior with positive reinforcement, just as we had used negative reinforcement for negative actions.

Meanwhile Sonic, Knuckles, and Tails were becoming more relaxed in the yard and less afraid of Baran. They would even come up to him from time to time and sniff noses. The next step was to walk around the yard with Baran on the leash and still muzzled. We didn't walk directly toward the bunnies, but rather sauntered about, encountering them from time to time. The bunnies did startle at first, and darted off. Baran flinched towards them but then corrected himself, and we praised him for this.

After a few of these sessions we were ready to let him go off leash. We kept the muzzle on with the thinking that even if he did revert to his basic instincts off leash, we would have time to rescue the bunny. In fact, if Baran had made such a move at this point we probably would have given up the attempt at such close-quarters integration. We knew we were asking a lot of him. But Baran's behavior was very gentlemanly.

We sat back and observed closely and would warn him from a distance if he was doing anything objectionable. We allowed him to walk behind the bunnies if he wanted to, especially since he had acquired a taste for bunny droppings, but we didn't let him move up on them quickly, out of fear it would develop into a chase situation. The real test came when Sonic ran up to Baran as he was sitting, saw him, and then ran off in the other direction. I could tell that Baran thought about giving chase (even if just in a playful mode), but he restrained himself and looked at me. He had learned to look to us for guidance. This stellar behavior won him more praise.

Finally, the big leap of faith: no leash, no muzzle. Thankfully, it was a non-event, and nothing really changed. When we added Peppy back into the mix, he seemed a bit confused at first as to why there were bunnies in the yard and yet they weren't being treated as prey, but he followed Baran's lead and did not go into hunting mode. Now we can all sit out in the yard on a nice day

Tails of the backyard: Free-running in their supervised yard, Tails and Baran pause to refresh at their respective water bowls.

and co-exist peacefully. This is by no means a daily activity, but a special outdoor time that we do when we have time to supervise. It's not so much that we worry about the dogs' behavior in our absence, but rather what the bunnies might do, such as chew on things they shouldn't or dig holes under the fence.

It's ironic that now the bunnies run away from us but not from the dogs, because they know that when we approach them it means that it's time to go back inside. ■

Bill Harriman, Ph.D., a molecular biologist, works in South San Francisco and lives with his family in Alameda, California.

Rabbits with Rabbits

Heights of love: Oliver presents himself to Penelope on whatever level is required.

RABBITS ARE EXTREMELY SOCIABLE—so much so, that our House Rabbit Society fosterers don't even adopt to homes where the rabbit will live in solitude (e.g., a backyard hutch).

Even though they are naturally sociable, rabbits don't always know this important fact about themselves. Or maybe they have forgotten this truth through the process of being domesticated and living in separate quarters. When rabbits live with other rabbits, neutering is essential. While spayed/neutered rabbits may be considered less "natural," they are, in actuality, able to enjoy a more natural lifestyle, since they can run about freely together and work out social structures.

When given a choice rabbits live naturally in groups, yet some are much more monogamous than others, and living as bonded pairs is more natural for them. After working on bonding solutions for many rabbits for many years, I introduce individuals based on personality rather than gender breed, or size.

RABBIT SEXUAL PSYCHOLOGY

We start with rabbits who are neutered or spayed. Hormones get in the way. Rabbits will mount each other regardless, and they don't need extra agitation. Don't assume that rabbit sexual activity ends with sterilization. Newly introduced rabbits often engage in a passionate courtship (which is preferable to a combative relationship). Rabbit sexuality is largely a mental attitude.

Why should the female be spayed if the male is neutered? Aside from many health reasons, this is the scenario. She will be mounted by the neutered male for the first day. Then suddenly her mood changes as she enters a false pregnancy. She rejects his advances and busies herself with destructive (to your house) activities, shredding paper and maybe curtains to build her nest. Meanwhile, he can't understand why she continuously has a "headache." She won't receive his amorous advances for another month. Neutered pairs have more fun than that.

Sometimes a rabbit mounts another backwards. This may be part of the seductive foreplay, but it can be quite risky for the rabbit on top if the rabbit under-

PHOTO: JIM STONEBURNER

neath is uncooperative. I'm sure that veterinarians who repair the damage consider it the malicious intent by one rabbit to amputate the genitals of another. (More likely it is a defense gesture by the rabbit on the bottom.) Whenever you see backwards mounting, you must intervene to protect the top bunny.

INTRODUCTORY STEPS

When introducing rabbits to each other, I make two assumptions. Yes, the rabbits will hate each other at first sight and, yes, they will become bonded friends. The second assumption for me is a matter of experience. For a beginner it's a matter of faith. Admittedly, there are times during the introduction process that I, too, would give up if I didn't know better.

The advice I give is to prepare for the worst, and if you have an easier time, so much the better. The materials you will need are, a water bottle with a spray pump and some neutral territory (any space that neither rabbit owns). This can be an enclosed porch or any small room, but the most successful in recent years is a "bonding pen" (page 16). Since the previous edition, I have once again revised my techniques for bonding rabbits. While we had no mishaps with the car rides that I used to recommend, we found that they were unnecessary, and at some point could have been unsafe (no seat belts on bonding rabbits).

THESE ARE THE STEPS:

Step 1. For the first few days let your bunnies get used to each other's presence. Use two separate living spaces, not necessarily side by side, but in the same room, where they can become acquainted with each other's scent. Exercise them in separate areas during the day.

Step 2. For the next few days, set up a pen with a litterbox and maybe a few toys. Put the bunnies into the pen and climb into it yourself. Hold a squirt bottle, set to "stream," and be ready to use it. Keep in spraying distance at all times, and if you see one rab-

PHOTOS: CAROLYN LONG

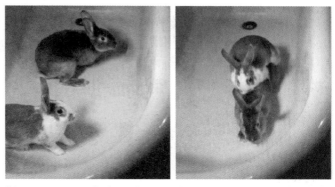

First Date: Suitable neutral territory for the introduction of this neutered pair is a Madison, Wisconsin bathtub.

bit start to attack the other, let him have it right in the face. He/she will take time out to face wash. This triggers another interesting behavior in the acceptance process. (I know this from videotaping many introductions.) When you see newly introduced rabbits simply occupying the same territory, apparently ignoring each other but nervously grooming themselves, you can bet that it won't be long, maybe a day or two, before they are grooming each other.

Sit with the bunnies each day for about 20 minutes, giving them your undivided attention. Don't allow a pattern of fighting. If they're not ready to play nice on any given day, then separate them until the next day or later the same day.

Step 3. As soon as the bunnies are able to tolerate each other for a full 20 minutes with you inside the pen, you can begin to position yourself outside the pen but stay nearby with the water bottle. (If the intended couple is not highly charged to begin with, you may not need to use the water bottle.) You can begin multi-tasking—pour yourself a beverage or write a few notes. My husband and I often have breakfast next to bonding bunnies.

Step 4. Increase the pen time until the bunnies are together most of the day. They may sit on oppo-

Wall o' rabbits. *This New Mexico sanctuary group can choose to bunch up or spread out (or up) according to mood.*

site sides of the pen at first. Gradually you will see them sitting closer together, then snuggling together during the day. Give them a few more days to firmly establish this cordial habit, then they are ready to share a bed and can remain together at night.

The whole process usually takes about five weeks. If your bunnies have had a head start with an introduction at the shelter, you can skip steps 1 and 2, and possibly 3. If you start with step 4, keep a supervisory eye on them for a while.

WHY GRADUAL?

Although friendship supports longevity in rabbits, introductions can be stressful to the immune system. Falling in love is one of life's most joyous experiences. But could anyone stand those butterflies in the stomach forever? Fortunately most creatures settle in to a comfortable relationship in time. When rabbits are first introduced, the "butterfly" period sometimes results in loose bowels. And in their excitement, most "honeymooners" temporarily forsake their good toilet habits, so you will have some extra cleanup for a couple of days.

Whenever we introduce older, chronically ill, or in any way compromised animals, we use extreme caution—in much the same way that gradual dietary changes are made, little bit at a time. Why introduce them at all? The potential for a positive and mutually beneficial relationship, if done gradually, outweighs the risk. The reason I proceed slowly in introducing all rabbits is to keep from overtaxing any immune system that might be fighting a subclinical disease in a seemingly healthy rabbit.

An interesting note is that rabbits in advancing years may accept partners who would have been intolerable at an earlier time (just as ill-suited younger humans find love in their golden years).

RABBITS IN GROUPS

In my own rabbit sanctuary, I prefer to keep rabbits in trios or small groups rather than pairs. This not only allows more rabbits into my house, but also minimizes the loneliness when one passes on. They have each other for comfort.

Putting together a group of rabbits is usually easier than introducing two individuals at a time. This may be due to a natural tendency of rabbits to fall into a hierarchical structure. Group introductions, up to about seven rabbits, can be handled generally the same way as for singles. With very large groups, it's not always possible to find neutral territory that hasn't already been claimed by one or two of the resident rabbits.

Rabbit rescuers who work with large group housing generally don't worry about neutral territory, but they do provide a larger space for the introduction, such as an entire backyard. They have a water hose ready, in case of serious fighting, but generally they rely on the rabbits' innate ability to structure a hierarchy. ∎

PHOTO: MARGO DEMELLO

Lifting and Handling

We lift our rabbits because it is necessary. We handle them because it is good for them. We get to know their physical makeup and take better care of them.

Left: Rusty is supported at his forelegs and rump, while being lifted up and out of a side door.
Inset: Roger is carried with rump and chest support.

PHOTOS: AMY ESPIE

Lifting with Confidence

Y OU WILL PROBABLY DISCOVER that Bunny does not particularly like to be picked up and carried around. All rabbits are a joy to watch, but not all are a joy to pick up. Your bunny may enjoy cozying up beside you, but being lifted and carried is a different matter. However, there are times when you must pick up your rabbit—to remove him from danger or take her to a veterinarian.

For this reason I recommend a daily exercise in lifting and handling by just picking her up and setting her down again. A brief, non-stressful lift followed by a small reward will help a rabbit overcome the fear of being lifted. Our formerly reluctant Phoebe caught on quickly. She soon began to circle my feet, tripping me, if I forgot her treat when I set her down.

Two positions that I use are shoulder-rump and feet-to-chest. I lift all large rabbits by the shoulders and rump.

BIG BUNNY LIFT

To pick up a large rabbit from the floor. Walk up confidently, get behind him, put one hand under the chest and one under the rump and lift, with au-

thority. Don't act timid. My technique is to hold the hindquarters firm and low to prevent kicking. My veterinarian does just the opposite, with the bunny rolled into a ball. Either way seems to prevent the feet from getting into kicking position.

Caution must be used in setting bunny back down. This is a time that they often leap in anticipation. If you feel your bunny kicking right out of your arms, drop into an immediate squat on the floor. Reducing the height will reduce the chances of injury to your bunny or yourself.

SMALL BUNNY LIFT

Smaller rabbits are usually better picked up from the front. They tend to feel more secure with their front feet resting on your collarbone or braced against your body for support. Place one hand under the forelegs and one hand under the rump and bring towards your body.

This lifting method is often the one that works best for children (over 8 years old), since they are better able to use their whole body for support of the bunny.

UP AND OUT

Rabbits can be lifted from a top-opening cage or pen the same way as from the floor. Top-opening doors are much easier for you than side-opening doors. The hardest lifting situation that you can possibly attempt is to pull a rabbit, of any size, through a small side-opening door. To get bunny out, reach in and place your hands on top of bunny's head, stroke him from head to tail, then scoop him toward you. The trick is to get your body close enough for him to get a footing with his front paws (see page 49). This will make him secure enough to be pulled out the rest of the way. ■

PHOTOS: BOB HARRIMAN

Socializing by Mutual Agreement

RABBITS ARE SOCIABLE CREATURES. They interact with toys, with each other, and with other animals. People who live with rabbits in a household are very eager to have these naturally sociable creatures interact with humans. How do you encourage this interactivity? Certainly not by sticking the rabbit off in a hutch, where she becomes bored and "boring." Include her in your daily life. If you are away at work all day, proximity should be a priority when you are home.

HUMAN ROUTINES

Predictable human behavior helps your bunny feel secure. How else does know what to expect? Show her that you have habits, too. She will see how nicely she fits in, especially when you are passing out the veggies or tossing her a wire ball (with a bell inside). If she nudges it and bumps it back, you can start a game of "catch." Some bunnies also enjoy a chase-the-towel game with their human playmates. Playing together is a form of communication that may well establish the groundwork for other interaction.

Rabbits choose to sit close to each other. To cozy up with you, let Bunny initiate it. Occupy the same space then do homework, read a book, or watch TV. She will come to you because it's the natural thing to do. She will investigate you as she does the other objects in her environment. There is no need

Fellowship of the floor: Some of the best things happen in low places. Nim gives affection-nuzzle to her human, Charlie (right).
Sharing snacks and moments of contentment, 3-year-old Will indulges eager Dorothy in treats she deserves (below).

to grab, hold, restrain, or coax her into your lap. We tell this to children often, and it is one of the most important things for a human of any age to know about their bunnies.

As she nudges and sniffs, she may hop onto your lap in due time. A towel across your lap will make it more inviting to your bunny, and you will be glad it's between you and the toenails that are trying to get a foothold. Let her hop on

PHOTOS: UPPER, AMY ESPIE; LOWER, HUGH DOUGLAS

"When handling rabbits, protect yourself with a barrier of clothing!"

and off your lap at will. When handling rabbits, protect yourself with a barrier of clothing! Don't blame your bunny for trying to get a secure toenail grip.

HEARING IS BELIEVING

Although rabbits do not often vocalize, they are happy to listen to a friendly human voice. The first way to socialize with a new bunny in your home is to have a lengthy phone conversation with a friend. Talk to, at, and around your bunny.

I discovered this fact several years ago after picking up five new rabbits from the animal shelter. They waited in cages in the living room while I scheduled neuter appointments. I had other business to attend and spent most of the afternoon on the phone, which was also in the living room. About two hours into the afternoon, I glanced around to find every one of the rabbits not only stretched out in relaxation but rolled over in euphoria.

Many bunnies also appreciate music. As you get better acquainted, you will learn what her tastes are.

HAND WORKS

Our hands are useful tools, but in the beginning stages of a relationship, hands are not always the best means to earn a rabbit's trust. Try communicating as a rabbit does—nose to nose. And when your rabbit is getting acquainted with you,

Deeply felt experience. Don Wild of San Francisco (right), who lives with multiple rabbits, pays with a pound of flesh for taking the toenail risk. **Summer-wear** *offers little protection when bunny is climbing on a human lap. Amy Harriman takes a precautionary measure (left). A cloth should be spread across all bare laps before exposure.*

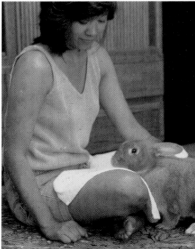

think of how your hand gestures may be interpreted. Is the approaching hand a threat or a giver of rewards? You must make it clear what your intentions are. When you are stroking a rabbit for the first time, approach directly from the top of the head, not under the chin.

Since hands can be visually frightening, let her feel the stroke of your hand on her head and down

PHOTOS: LEFT, MARINELL HARRIMAN; RIGHT, JANIS WILD

"...think of how your gestures may be interpreted."

her back before attempting the lower parts of the face. Rabbits groom each other around the eyes, top of the nose, top of the head, ears, and down the back. Stroking them in these areas feels friendly.

TOUCH THERAPY

Most of us probably began as small children to meet our need to fondle something "cute" by petting our companion animals. As we grew older, we learned that stroking an animal is good for us. It lowers our blood pressure. We have used our animals to make ourselves feel better. They are soothing to us after a hard day's work.

Now, we are learning that, with a little training, we can turn our need to pet into something beneficial for our companions. Stroking and touching animals is being used increasingly in therapy along with veterinary medicine. Some of the more popular and effective techniques include massage, acupressure, T-touch, shamanic healing, reiki, and many others. Do a Web search for details.   ■

Learning Kindness From Rabbits

By Margo DeMello, Ph.D.

Numerous studies have shown that there is a link between the abuse of animals and violence towards humans; that children who engage in animal cruelty are more likely to commit violent acts as adults.

Scientists and animal advocates are now finding that the corollary may be true as well: children raised in an environment in which animals are loved and nurtured may grow up to be nurturing, compassionate adults.

The research on this subject is not yet conclusive, but we do know that parents play a major role in the development of humane attitudes in children by exposing them to pets and teaching them, by example, loving care. We also know that there is a positive correlation between having companion animals as a child and developing a concern about the welfare of other animals.

But does this necessarily translate into a concern for humans as well? Since the Victorian era, parents have been bringing home pets to teach kindness to children, in the understanding that children who bond with animals als will develop empathy towards humans, and new research is beginning to confirm this. What is most intriguing about this new research is that the type of animal one lives with, and the level of bond one forms, may play a large part in this.

No one has studied the relationship between children (or adults) and their rabbits, or how it may correlate to how rabbit caretakers feel about others, but from knowing hundreds of rabbit lovers, I can make a couple of guesses.

First, I think that living with a house rabbit teaches us kindness towards other animals. *Countless rabbit people have changed how they eat, how they dress, and what products they buy, as they become aware that there is no real difference between the rabbits forced to endure the laboratory and the slaughterhouse, and the beloved companions living in their homes. It seems that for many rabbit caretakers, their love for their rabbits is globalized to include other animals. But do we take our love and extend it to humanity as well?*

There's no way to know for sure, but certainly the hundreds of House Rabbit Society volunteers use their love of rabbits to not just help rabbits, but to help people as well, forming connections that are deep, meaningful and worldwide.   ■

Margo DeMello, Ph.D. *is co-author of* Stories Rabbits Tell. *She teaches sociology in Albuquerque, New Mexico.*

Biting Words

ONE PART OF BUNNY VOCABULARY that people most often misinterpret is biting. By observing "rabbit rules of etiquette" (described on page 12) and by understanding the occasions in which bunny uses "bite-words," you can avoid having these conversations. Here are a few of the occasions and ways to circumvent them.

Testing. It's common for baby rabbits to go through a period of testing their teeth. If your bunny decides to test his teeth on you, I advise a small screech. This is a sound rabbits make in dire distress. He will understand that this is serious business.

Move-over. Rabbits may nip whatever is in their way. It can be another rabbit who is blocking the water bottle or a human arm that is confining a rabbit to a lap. Screeching may work, but it might be better to avoid using your arm or any part of your body as a barricade.

Zealous grooming. When grooming each other, rabbits pull out burrs and chew foreign particles entangled in each other's fur. Keep this in mind when your rabbit friend is licking your sleeve or pant leg and comes to a seam or wrinkle that could be interpreted as foreign and therefore removable.

Defense. As stated earlier, objects coming from below eye level may appear threatening. Don't stick your hand up to a rabbit's nose to be sniffed as you would to a dog or scratch under the chin as you would a cat. Your extremities, hands or feet, may be judged separately from the rest of yourself, so don't assume that your bunny doesn't like you if he distrusts your hands. It may take a while to connect those foreign objects to you.

Side approach. A human hand is all the more threatening to a shy rabbit when it is reaching in through a small side-opening cage door. As you invade her safe haven, she backs into the far corner, forcing you to approach her from the front at eye level. You must find a way to approach from the top, even if it means installing a new top-opening door or enlarging the one on the side.

Aromatic fingers. If you have been eating pretzels or dicing carrots, don't stick your fingers immediately into bunny's cage.

Possessiveness. Unspayed females (or unneutered males) may be particularly protective with their possessions, and it's best to clean the cage when it is unoccupied.

Misdirection. A human referee may incur a misdirected bite for trying to intervene between two rabbit adversaries—in much the same way that a person gets scratched by grabbing a cat from an attacking dog. You might also have same negative results when you carry the scent of a "foreign" rabbit on your clothing.

I have to comment on rabbits labeled "biters." The best way to "cure" aggression in a rabbit is to redirect the energy by meeting animosity with benevolence. When aggression is channeled into affection, the bite becomes a lick. Some of my most affectionate rabbits are converted biters.

For instance, every time we walked into his room, our rabbit Bandit would come lunging and growling to bite our ankles, only to find himself getting a thorough rub-down, hair brushing, flea combing, or massages behind the ears. His lunges soon became exuberant greetings accompanied by a silly dance.

The assertive rabbit may always need to assert. But when the urge to attack is combined with a fondness for the attacked, the bite attack is replaced by an affection attack, which is just as gratifying as having a dog meet you at the door. It's well worth your effort to establish a loving relationship with an aggressive-affectionate rabbit. ■

Feeding for Longevity

Not only do we consider what to feed our rabbits for their individual needs but also the condition of the particular foods we choose for them.

Left: Nibble samples a basil leaf from her human's salad plate.
Inset: Rosaline Ng of Hong Kong shares an enzyme tablet with her bunny Toto.

PHOTOS: ABOVE, BOB HARRIMAN; INSET, MICKEY FAN

Appropriate Foods

W E USE FOOD TO WIN our rabbits' friendship. We bribe them with edible gifts and encourage them to beg for a treat. We enjoy seeing them full-bellied and satisfied—until we are told that they are overweight.

Domestic rabbits, like their wild cousins, are able to consume large quantities of organic material. Wild rabbits eat succulent grass in the spring, dried grass or straw later in the year. They eat cultivated crops grown for feedstuffs and garden vegetables grown for humans. They eat the fruit that falls from trees, as well as bark from the trees themselves. At times, wild rabbits must survive on twigs and shrubs that are nutritionally low quality to other animals. To do this, they must consume a large volume and convert it to higher quality protein and energy.

Rabbits are voracious eaters, and they also love to forage. This is built in to their survival instinct. Feeding your house rabbit is more than fulfilling nutritional requirements. You are feeding a little psyche—not only in a bowl but also by stashing those high-bulk, low-calorie chewables around the house for bunny to find. That's part of the program.

INDIGESTIBLE FIBER

As much as your bun needs digestible organic material, he also needs a large quantity of indigestible fiber. Hay provides both of these. However, alfalfa and clover hays are usually too high in calcium and protein to be given in large quantities to mature non-breeding rabbits, in conjunction with pellets. On the other hand, nutritional values in dried hays vary greatly with the season and the cut—making it difficult to meet protein requirements consistently with hay alone.

Wild rabbits have access to many forages that meet their protein needs, but these are not normally found in the grocery store (like the inner bark of a maple tree). A grass-based hay is usually best for mature rabbits, because of its lower protein and calcium content. However, hay is so critical to good health that it's better to feed alfalfa and clover-based hays, rather than no hay at all. Choose long-strand hays to obtain the maximum fiber benefit, and keep all hay dry. Mold can kill a rabbit.

FRESH PRODUCE

Veggies: Most of what you find in the produce section of the supermarket is OK for your rabbit, with a few exceptions. Avoid starchy vegetables (corn, potatoes, beans), as these can cause digestive upset. Do offer a variety of vegetables and include a range of lettuces, fresh herbs, brassicas (broccoli family), and other greens. Some rabbits have sensitivities to certain vegetables, so test them one at a time when introducing them into your rabbit's diet.

Never offer a rabbit raw beans, potato peels, rhubarb, avocado, or any scraps that are too old to eat yourself. Spoiled food might make you sick, but it could kill your rabbit.

Fruit: Fresh apples, pears, peaches, plums, pineapples, papayas, grapes, and bananas are favorites with rabbits, and I find them useful for

PHOTO: QUAK WAN-LING

camouflaging oral medications. While refined sugar, as in candy or cookies, should never be offered, adult rabbits are able to digest fructose, or fruit sugar, extremely well (Buddington 1990). Therefore, fresh fruit can be given safely (no pits or seeds), but watch bunny's weight if fruit is a large part of her diet.

PELLET COMPOSITION

One reason you might choose to feed pellets, in small amounts, is that you're not able to provide a wide enough variety of whole foods to meet nutrient requirements, which are *more* than adequately met with commercial rabbit feeds. Pellet ingredients are listed on the bag in their order of abundance. These ingredients are formulated to arrive at the percentages, also listed on the bag, of protein, fiber, and additional vitamins and minerals. Calories, or digestible energy (DE), are not always listed. Given in limited amounts, pellets can ensure adequate nutrition, but when given in excess, pellets can cause obesity. Their "shelf life" can be as long as 6 months if stored in a cool dry place.

Pellets were developed for livestock, with an emphasis on rapid weight gain, but some manufacturers produce "maintenance" varieties. In choosing a pellet, look for one that is lower in protein, calcium, and energy, and higher in fiber. Several manufacturers now produce pellets made with grass hay instead of alfalfa. There are also alfalfa-based pellets that are lower in protein and high in fiber. Avoid pellet mixes that contain whole seeds, grains and dried vegetables, because these are calorie-rich and many rabbits learn to prefer these at the expense of other foods.

Grains: Oats and barley in very small amounts are digestible to rabbits but can lead to weight or digestive problems. Avoid crackers, seeds, nuts, or fried banana, which are high in starch, sugars, or fats. Excess starch and sugar will wind up in the cecum (page 67), where they can cause very serious illness or even death. ■

Table 1: *Energy, protein, fiber, and calcium in several feedstuffs per one-ounce servings*

FRESH PRODUCE	DRY MAT. (%)	ENERGY (calories)	PROTEIN (%)	PROTEIN (g)	FIBER (%)	FIBER (g)	CALCIUM (%)	CALCIUM (mg)
Apple	21	20	0.5	.1	1.2	.3	.01	3
Banana	24	24	1.1	.3	.5	.1	.01	3
Broccoli	9.3	8.0	3.0	0.8	1.1	0.3	.05	13
Cabbage	12	8	2.2	.6	2.0	0.6	.08	23
Carrot tops	17	—	2.7	.8	1.9	0.5	.32	91
Carrots	12	14	1.2	.3	1.1	0.3	.04	11
Celery	6	4	0.9	.3	.6	0.2	.04	11
Chard, swiss	7.3	5.6	1.8	0.5	0.8	0.24	0.05	15
Cilantro	7.2	7.0	2.4	0.7	0.8	0.21	0.1	28
Collards	9.4	5.3	1.6	0.44	0.6	0.16	9.12	33
Dandelion greens	15	8	2.8	.8	1.7	0.5	.20	57
Endive	6.2	4.0	1.25	0.3	0.9	0.35	0.05	13
Kale	15	9	3.1	.9	2.0	0.6	.24	68
Lettuce, green	5	3	1.2	.3	.6	0.2	.05	14
Parsley	11.6	—11.0	3.0	0.9	1.2	0.36	.09	41
Spinach	8.4	6.0	2.7	0.8	2.5	0.7	0.1	28
HAYS & GRAINS								
Alfalfa hay	90	51	15.3	4.3	27.0	7.7	1.35	383
Bermuda grass hay	92	47	11.0	3.1	27.6	7.8	.38	108
Clover hay red	88	50	17.3	4.9	21.8	6.2	1.28	364
Clover hay white	92	58	21.4	6.1	20.9	5.9	1.75	497
Lespedeza hay	92	37	12.7	3.6	28.1	8.0	.92	261
Oats grain	90	77	11.1	3.2	11.3	3.2	.03	9
Oat hay	88	57	7.3	2.1	29.5	8.4	.25	71
Orchard grass fresh	27	15	3.8	1.1	6.9	2.0	.07	20
Prairie hay	92	47	5.3	1.5	31.0	8.8	.0	0
Ryegrass hay	89	59	3.8	1.1	33.0	9.4	.45	128
Sunflower seeds	92	94	17.1	4.9	22.3	6.3	.20	57
Timothy hay	80	57	6.3	1.8	30.2	8.6	.20	57
Wheat straw	89	38	3.2	.9	37.0	10.5	.15	43

Reference
Table 1 is adapted from Rabbit Feeding and Nutrition (Cheeke 1987) with specifically rabbit values unless otherwise noted.

ANY DIET PLAN should be appropriate to age and metabolism. Dietary needs for most species change with maturity. Mature rabbits tend to gain weight while geriatric rabbits sometimes have trouble maintaining weight. Any diet plan should be appropriate to age and metabolism.

THE YOUNG DIET

Take extra care with weanlings, under 7 weeks old, to keep their food clean. This is a transition period, in which the sterile intestines are being introduced to bacteria. Rabbits must establish healthy intestinal flora in order to survive. (For hand feeding orphan babies see chapter 10.)

Table 2. *Beginner Diets: Babies and "Teenagers."*

Birth to 2 weeks	mother's milk
2 to 4 weeks	Mother's milk, nibbles of alfalfa hay, pellets, well washed greens—introduced one at a time (Orphans: baby food starter, see page 85)
4 to 7 weeks	Mother's milk, alfalfa hay, pellets, well washed veggies/fruit—introduced one at a time
7 weeks to 7 mo.	Unlimited alfalfa hay, some pellets, additional veggies/fruit—one at a time
7 mo. to one year	Introduce grass and oat hays, gradually eliminate alfalfa, limit or eliminate pellets, expand variety of fresh produce

THE ADULT DIET

Since mature rabbits tend toward obesity, they require less of everything—except fiber. Your job is to try keep your bunny's minimum requirements met but not to excess.

You need a kitchen or postal scale in order to put together a diet of mixed ingredients while ensuring adequate nutrition. Raw leafy vegetables don't weigh a lot. Throw a handful of dandelion greens on the kitchen scale and you only get an ounce. A large handful of hay is about two ounces. To get three ounces you need about a shoebox full.

If your rabbit is reluctant to eat the hay that's available to her at all times, try having two different kinds available alternately. This way you can give fresh offerings of one kind then the other, or even fresh offerings of the same hay. When I come around in the afternoon, and offer my rabbits the same kind of hay that they're sitting on, they grab it from my hand like it's a big deal.

Table 3. *Sample Diet for Mature Rabbits*

Vegetables:	Varied and mixed 4-6 oz daily
Fresh fruit:	(Omit if overweight) 1/2 oz daily
Grass hay:	Unlimited, but encourage at least 3 oz.
Pellets:	1/8 cup daily (to ensure trace amounts of vital nutrients. Adjust according to needs)

Because pellets range widely in their caloric content, you should adjust the serving size to your rabbit's individual needs. In general, smaller rabbits need more food per pound that do larger rabbits. ■

Table 4: *Minimal Metabolic Requirements for Rabbits to Maintain Optimum Body Weight*

Body wt lbs	2	3	4	5	6	7	8	9	10
Calories	89	120	149	170	202	227	251	274	296

Reference
Based on average of several studies estimating maintenance requirements of New Zealand Whites (Cheeke 1987,70-71)

PHOTOS: LEFT, BOB HARRIMAN; RIGHT, JIM STONEBURNER

Special Diets for Special Needs

CERTAIN CONDITIONS REQUIRE diet adjustments. For some bunnies, a special diet may be no more than adding a supplement, such as banana for extra potassium for the kidneys, or reduced salt for a heart patient, or of course reduced calories for weight reduction.

Some disabled rabbits need to be hand fed and may need to keep their weight and hydration up with a moist pellet mixture. Pureed "baby food" foods, such as pumpkin, squash, carrots, banana, plums, and applesauce, can be good supplements to boost calorie-intake for invalid rabbits.

PELLET PASTE

This mixture includes pellets and water, pulverized enough to slide through a feeding syringe. It is usually a temporary diet during convalescent care. The following formula is a 2-day supply for 6-pound rabbit:

1/2 rounded cup dry pellets
3/4 cup water
Soak pellets for 10 minutes,
Blend at high speed for 5 minutes.
Stir in supplements, such as pureed baby food.

Spoon the mixture into a 25cc feeding syringe from your vet. For a large rabbit, use two. The amount that can be fed at 4-5 hour intervals is about 50cc (for a 6-pound rabbit). Adjust to weight.

MOISTENED PELLETS FOR SENIORS

This is my favorite diet for feeble elderly rabbits, who need to keep their weight up. It ensures more fluid intake when they are unable to drink adequately on their own.

2 heaping tablespoons pellets
1/4 cup water (a little less with baby food)
1 oz baby food (optional)

Soak pellets, add supplements, then dump the mixture into a saucer. Keep the "mush" spooned into a mound that can be lapped up by bunny.

This feeding can be repeated 3-4 times a day. Veggies and hay are also desirable for frail seniors after their calorie needs are met with pellets.

HIGH-FLUID DIET

This may benefit bunnies with "sludge" urine or bladder stones. After our 6-year-old Colleen had a huge bladder stone removed, her veterinarian devised a high-fluid diet for her to keep her urine diluted. We gave Colleen subcutaneous Lactated Ringer's Solution twice daily, immediately after her surgery and then reduced it to twice a week as her diet did the dilution work.

Table 5. *Sample Diet for Sludge/Stones*

Leafy greens:	4 oz minimum
Root/stalk (carrot, celery, broccoli):	4 oz
Fresh fruit (e.g.,, apple slice):	1/2 oz
Grass hay:	Unlimited
Wet pellets:	1 tablespoon

I had to get used to the volume. As noted before, leafy greens don't weigh much. This meant finding a good source. I struck out with the supermarket (policies don't allow giving away their extra produce) but our local stand, Paul's Produce, in Alameda was quite helpful. I was given huge boxes of the outer leaves of romaine and butter lettuce, which gave the basic bulk. I purchased the other favorites—parsley, cilantro, celery, radish, carrots, and apples.

This diet did indeed give our 5 lb. Colleen an extra year of comfortable time and kept her USG (urine specific gravity) under 1.010. It was well worth the effort. In the process, I had to give all the other bunnies extra handfuls of veggies too. Their enthusiasm over these regular and expected offerings now give us excellent guidelines for knowing when appetites are off, and we can watch for other signs of illness. ∎

Obesity in Rabbits–
Loving Thumper to Death

BY SUSAN SMITH, Ph.D.

So you've fed thumper too many treat foods and unlimited pellets, and now your vet tells you that she's overweight. What do you do? Just as in humans, maintaining an ideal body weight is essential for your rabbit's good health. Obese rabbits find it difficult to reach their cecal pellets and clean themselves. Obesity places a heavy burden on the heart, can reduce cecum functions, and promotes diabetes and liver disease. In a medical emergency, excess body fat makes it difficult to predict your rabbit's response to anaesthesia. Obesity turns a routine surgery into a high-risk event.

It's easy for excess weight to sneak up. I recommend taking a photograph of your rabbit's side profile, and then compare it over the years. A healthy weight profile resembles the slim silhouette, whereas an overweight rabbit looks more like the dashed outlines. If in doubt, ask your vet, and be brave enough to accept her honest answer.

Just like people, rabbits should lose fat weight slowly and safely. That is, no more than 1-2% of their body weight should be lost per week. This means, for example, that it should take two and one half to five months (10 to 20 weeks) for five-pound Thumper to lose that extra pound. This slower weight reduction helps your rabbit to readjust her metabolism to this new diet. Exercise is critical for weight reduction as well.

How do you implement this new diet? First, switch to a grass-based rather than an alfalfa- based pellet, because these have a lower caloric density. If not available in your area, ask your pet food store to stock it, or order directly on the Internet. Be sure to mix the new and old pellets initially, and reduce the

FIGURE 8-1: Potential Areas of Obesity

Photograph your bunny's profile at a slim young age and compare it over the years. Fat may accumulate in the outlined areas.

volume gradually, so your rabbit has time to adjust. Use a measuring cup when dispensing pellets and follow the feeding guidelines. Offer unlimited grass hay so that Thumper has something to snack on between meals. Add fresh vegetables to the daily diet, and add new ones individually so her gut adjusts to these changes. Use fresh vegetables as a treat, instead of sugary or starchy foods. Carefully monitor your rabbit's weight and keep a written record of it.

By giving Thumper time to adjust to her new diet, both she and you will be rewarded with good health and a more active companion. ∎

Susan Smith, Ph.D. is Professor, Department of Nutritional Sciences, University of Wisconsin-Madison, with a Ph.D. in Biochemistry.

Plants Not for Chewing

HOUSE AND GARDEN PLANTS are chewing temptations, but domestic rabbits do not know by instinct which to avoid. When you think your rabbit may have consumed something poisonous, you must take immediate action. However, you can save yourself this anxiety if you learn what you have in your house and yard and remove/give away anything too dangerous for your bunny to eat.

The following list has been researched in-depth and divided into levels of toxicity. As more is learned about rabbit-specific toxic plants, the information will be posted on the Web <www.rabbit.org>.

Toxicity Classes

BY GEORGE FLENTKE, Ph.D.

Not all species or varieties of these plants has the same levels of toxins. Classification is based on the most dangerous plant of that species or variety.

An example is the Avocado. Avocados are of several varieties, only one of which contains toxins at dangerous levels to species other than humans. Hybridization of the varieties for agricultural reasons has made it difficult to determine if the toxic variety is part of a hybrid species. Thus all avocados are assumed to be problematic.

Many plants are safe if treated to destroy toxins. Fruit trees are all listed as Class 1 toxins, but if the bark and branches are totally dried out, the toxins are destroyed. The sticks make wonderful rabbit chew toys. Remember if the sticks have any green in the bark (scrape through with a fingernail), then they are not dried. The seeds of all pit fruits, apples and pears should be treated as Class 1 toxins even if dried.

Class 1: Universal species toxins, these are usually systemic toxins or local effect toxins of sufficient intensity to cause systemic problems. In general these plants should not be part of your household, or they should be well protected from rabbits. (Continued)

CLASS ONE

Anenome
Angel's trumpet
Apple
Apricot
Arrowgrass
Autumn crocus
Avocado
Azalea
Baby wood rose
Balsam apple
Balsam pear
Baneberry (white, red, black)
Beafsteak plant
Bittersweet
Bitterweed
Black cherry
Black nightshade
Bladderpod
Bloodroot
Blue gum
Bluebonnet
Boxwood
Buddhist pine
Bunchberry
Buttercup/ Ranuncula
Butterfly weed
Calico bush/ Moutain laurel
California holly

Carolina jasmine
Castor bean
Chalice vine
Cherry laurel
Chinese bellflower
Chinese lantern
Chokecherry
Christmas berry
Christmas rose
Cocklebur
Coytillo
Crowpoison
Daffodil
Daphne
Day-blooming jessamine
Deadly nightshade
Death Camas
Delphinium
Devil's tomato
Dieffenbachia
Doll's eyes
Dumbcane
Elderberry
English ivy
English laurel
European nightshade
Exotica perfection

False parsley
False wild grape
Flowering maple
Flypoison
Fool's parsley
Foxglove
Fruit pits
Glory lily
Gold dieffenbachia
Goldenchain
Goldenrain
Greasewood
Halogeton
Hawaiian baby wood rose
Helebore
Henbane
Horse nettle
Indian hemp
Indian tobacco
Indigo
Inkberry
Inkweed/ Drymary
Jasimine
Jequirity beans
Jerusalem cherry
Jessamine
Jimmy fern/ Cloak fern

Jimson weed/ Thorn apple
Jonquil
Karela
Laburnum
Lambkill
Larkspur
Leucaena
Ligustrum
Lillies
Lily-of-the-valley
Lobelia
Lupines
Mandrake
May apple
Meadow saffron
Mescal
Milk vetch
Milkweed
Molds in hay
Monkshood
Moonflower
Moonseed
Morning glory
Mother-in-law plant
Mountain laurel
Mushrooms
Needlepoint ivy
Nutmeg
Oleander
Orange sneezeweed

Paradise plant
Peach tree
Pear tree
Perill mint
Periwinkle
Peyote
Pheasant's eye
Plum tree
Poison ash
Poison hemlock
Poison ivy
Poison nut
Poison oak
Poison sumac
Poke salad
Pokeweed
Poppy
Potato
Precatory bean
Prickly poppy
Privet hedge
Purple mint
Red sage
Rhododendron
Ripple ivy
Rosary pea
Rose-bay
Scilla
Sheep laurel
Silverleaf nightshade
Sneezeweed

Spider climbing lily
Spotted dumb cane
Squill
Stinkweed
Swamp laurel/ Bog laurel
Sweetheart ivy
Tansy
Toadstools
Tomato
Toyon
Trumpet flower
Trumpet plant
Tullidora
Variable dieffenbachia
Water hemlock
Water parsnip
Wild carrot
Wild cucumber
Wild jessamine
Wild mushrooms
Wild peas
Windflower
Wolfsbane
Wood-rose
Yellow jasmine
Yew
Yllis

"If you suspect a poisoning, call your veterinarian…"

Class 2: Local toxins (Allergens, dermal sensitivity) or systemic toxins of lesser strengths. Since rabbits inevitably chew items, these toxins could be more of a problem than the current literature indicates, and these plants should be viewed with caution.

Class 3: Low risk plants due to low level of toxins or toxins that herbivores, such as rabbits, routinely handle better than nonherbivore species. This class also contains plants that have historically been considered quite toxic, but recently whose toxicity is being reevaluated as nontoxic or low toxicity.

FOR SUSPECTED POISONING

Call your veterinarian. Bring in the whole suspected plant or chewed parts of plant. Check all plants to make sure that chewing is confined only to that plant.

Class 1: Report to your veterinarian immediately, or go to an emergency clinic.

Class 2: Call your veterinarian for consultation on whether an appointment is warranted.

Class 3: Watch rabbit carefully for any signs of poisoning or ill health. Call your veterinarian if you feel it is warranted. ■

George Flentke, Ph.D., at University Wisconsin-Madison with a Ph.D. in Biochemistry. Also, Manager of the Madison Chapter of the House Rabbit Society.

Toxicity Classes © 2005 by George Flentke.

CLASS TWO
African blue lily
Agapanthus
Alder buckthorn
Amaryllis
American hellebore
Anthurium
Arrowhead vine
Barberry
Bear grass
Begonia (sand)
Bird of paradise
Bleeding heart
Blue gum
Bracken fern
Buckeye/ Horse chesnut
Buckthorn
Burning bush
Cactus
Caladium
Calendula/ Pot marigold
Calla lily
Candelabra cactus
Cardinal flower
Carnations
Cassine
Century plant
Ceriman/ Split-leaf philodendron/ Mexican bread-fruit
Chinaberry tree
Chinese inkberry
Clematis
Climbing bittersweet
Coffee bean/ Senna bean
Coral berry/ Snowberry
Cordatum/ Philodendron
Corn cockle
Corn plant
Cow parsnip

Cowslip
Crinum lily
Croton
Crown of thorns
Crown vetch
Cut-leaf philodendron
Cycads
Cyclamen
Dasheen
Dessert tobacco
Devil's ivy
Dianthus
Dracaena palm/ Ribbon plant
Dutchman's breeches
Dutchman's pipe
Elephant ear
Emerald feather
Emerald fern
Eucalyptus
Euonymus
Everlasting pea
Eyebane
False hellebore
False sago palm
Fern palms
Fiddleneck
Fireweed
Fishtail palm
Florida beauty
Fruit salad plant
Geranium (California)
Gladiola
Gold dust dracaena
Golden pothos
Green cestrum
Green gold nephthysis
Guajillo
Hogweed
Hogwort
Horsebrush
Horsetail reed
Hunter's robe
Hyacinth

Hydrangea
Indian poke
Indian tobacco
Inkberry
Iris
Jack-in-the-pulpit
Japanese pagoda tree
Locoweed
Lucky bamboo
Madagascar dragon tree/ Red-margined dracaena
Marble queen
Marijuana
Marsh marigold
Meadow pea
Mesquite
Mexican bread-fruit
Minature croton
Mistletoe
Nephthytis/ Chinese evergreen
Night Jessamine
Oak tree
Panda
Paper-flowers
Partridge breast
Peace Lily
Pencil tree
Peony
Persian violet
Philodendron
Pigweed
Pingue/Colorado rubber weed
Plumosa fern
Poinciana
Pot mum/ Spider mum
Pothos
Prickly copper-weed
Pride of Barbados
Rabbitbrush

Rayless goldenrod
Red princess
Rhubarb
Sacahuista
Saddle leaf philodendron
Sago palm
Sand begonia
Satin pothos
Schefflera
Scindapus
Shamrock plant/ Oxalis
Silver pothos
Skunk cabbage
Snow-on-the-mountain
Solomon's seal
Spathe flower
Split leaf philodendron
Star of Bethlehem
Strawberry bush
Striped dracaena
Sweet flag
Sweet pea
Swiss cheese plant
Tallow, Chinese/ Japanese
Tansy
Tara
Taro vine
Tobacco
Tree philodendron
Tulip
Umbrella plant
Variegated philo-dendron
Variegated rubber plant
Walnut
Warneckei dracaena
White snakeroot
Wild tobacco
Wisteria
Yaupon holly

CLASS THREE
Acacia
African rue
Aloe vera
Alsike clover
Apple leaf croton
Asparagus fern
Baccharis
Betel nut palm
Black locust
Black root/black snakeroot
Black walnut
Blue cohosh
Boston ivy
Broomweed
Calamondin orange tree
Cineraria/ Groundsel
Creeping Charlie (not house-plant)
Cuban laurel
Daisy
Emerald duke
Fiddle-leaf fig
Firecracker
Firethorn
Fireweed
Four o'clock
Gentians
German ivy
Gill over the ground
Ginko
Goatweed
Ground ivy
Groundsel
Heart ivy
Heartleaf
Holly tree/bush
Horse-head
Indian laurel
Indian rubber plant
Johnson Grass
Juniper

Kafir
Klamath weed
Lechiguilla
Maiden hair tree
Majesty
Medicine plant
Milo
Poinsettia
Primrose
Purple sesbane
Pyracantha
Rattlebox
Rattleweed
Red emerald
Silverling
Snakeweed
Sorghum
Sprengeri fern (asparagus)
St. Johns wort
String of beads
String of pearls
Sudan grass
True aloe
Turpentine plant
Virginia creeper
Weeping fig
Wild cucumber/ Balsam apple
Wild pea
Woodbine
Yerba-de-pasmo

Conditions, Diagnosis, Treatment

Knowing the physical make-up and functions of your rabbit will help you prevent illness and get appropriate veterinary help when needed.

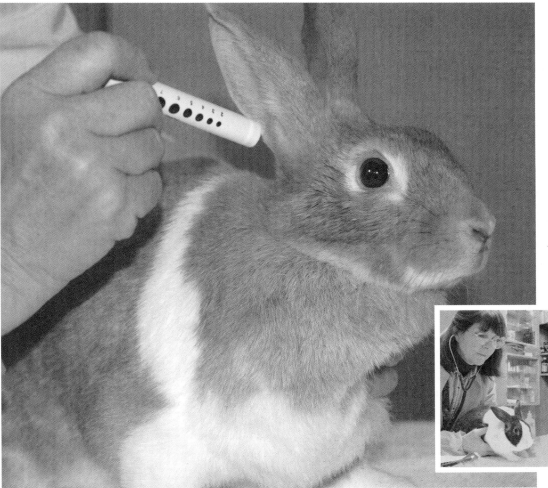

Left and inset:
Veterinary exams for incoming rabbits at the HRS Rabbit Center are donated by Dr. Carolynn Harvey.

Digestive Processing

THE RABBIT DIGESTIVE SYSTEM is truly amazing. If you make an effort to understand how it works, you will be able to prevent many illnesses that result from improper feeding.

INTESTINAL FORTITUDE

The standard churning and mixing process in the stomach is similar to that of other animals, but the intestines handle the food much differently.

The small intestine. The very long length of the rabbit small intestine is where most nutrients are absorbed. Sugars and starches are absorbed here and up to 90% of the ingested protein. Rabbits do not digest cellulose, or plant cells, efficiently in the small intestine, (Gidenne 1992) but they have an alternate way of dealing with this major part of their diet. Material passes from the small intestine to the cecum and colon. Then it is processed according to size.

THE CECUM

Contractions of the large fermenting vat, or cecum, keep large particles pushed out. Small particles of cellulose are retained for fermentation, along with excess sugar, starch and protein from the small intestine. Fermentation means digesting by bacteria. The cecum is filled with beneficial, food-digesting bacteria and protozoa.

THE COLON

The large intestine, or colon, does some unique things in rabbits. In addition to forming fecal pellets, it separates small particles in the haustral section and sends them backwards into the cecum. (Haustrae are sacculations formed by circular muscles.)

Large fiber particles are sent on their way from here for a quick passage through the colon to become the large hard marbles that you see in your bunny's litterbox. Contrary to what you might expect, the large particles don't get stuck inside the rabbit while the small ones exit easily. It's the other way around.

RECYCLING PLAN

The fermentation process in the cecum produces volatile fatty acids, which are absorbed directly into the bloodstream. The cecum also produces B-complex vitamins and protein to be reingested. The vitamin/protein-rich material from the cecum is packaged into little clusters of cecotropes while passing through the colon.

Cecotropes are an important part of your bunny's diet. They are enclosed in a mucus-membrane coating, which protects cecotrope bacteria from stomach acid, allowing them to ferment several more hours in the stomach after they are reingested. Finally the cecotropes are ready to pass to the small intestine where the nutrients are absorbed.

That's a pretty elaborate, round-about way of getting nourishment out of a blade of grass or the apple tree branch your bunny has been nibbling on (or your baseboard), but it works for wild rabbits who must get the most out of the poor food sources that are available.

In the wild, rabbits are not given a daily bowl of pellets that satisfy all of their nutritional requirements. Nature has designed for them a complicated plan of food processing and reprocessing, which depends on a digestive tract that is constantly moving.

LITTERBOX INDICATORS

Your bunny's digestion can be monitored via the litterbox. You should see regular dry round marbles. The following may indicate digestive trouble:

Excessive soft clusters (cecotropes), left unconsumed, may mean the diet is too protein rich.

Small hard scanty droppings mean less is coming through the GI tract

Strung marbles together in ropes of hair indicate excessive hair is being swallowed.

Watery diarrhea means digestion has shut down. ■

"...an elaborate, round-about way of getting nourishment..."

FIGURE 9-1:
Rabbit Gastrointestinal Tract

1. Esophagus. Plant food, ground in a sideways motion of the lower jaw, is swallowed and passed to the *stomach* through the esophagus.

2. Stomach. Muscular contractions squeeze and churn the food in a circular path, mixing them with the *gastric fluid* of the stomach, which is kept sterile by stomach acids.

3. Duodenum (first part of the *small intestine*). As the food particles exit the stomach, bile from the *liver* is secreted into the small intestine at the duodenum.

4. Small Intestine (comprised of the *duodenum, jejunum,* and *ileum*).The major part of digestion takes place during the passage through the small intestine. Some sugars, most starches, and up to 90% of all protein are absorbed, while *cellulose* is not efficiently digested.

5. Ileocecocolonic junction (major crossroads in the intestinal tract). Material passes from the small intestine to the *cecum* and *proximal colon*. Material also passes back and forth between the cecum and proximal colon in continual flux. (Cheeke 1987)

6. Cecum (fermenting vat). Contractions keep large particles moving into the colon. Small particles are retained for fermentation. Bacteria digest small-fiber cellulose, along with protein, sugars and starches that haven't been digested in the small intestine. B-complex vitamins are produced along

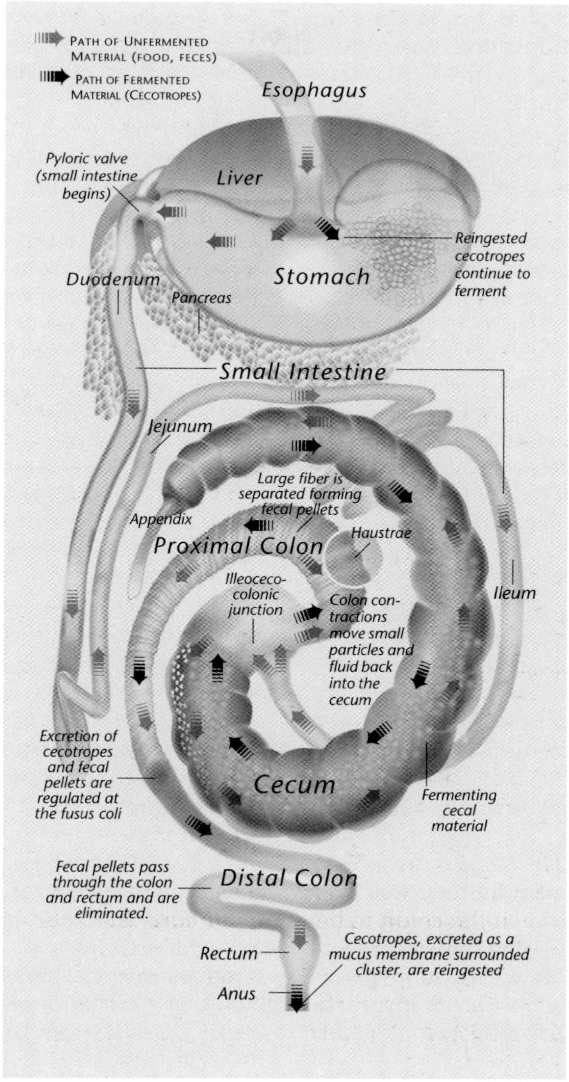

with volatile fatty acids, which are absorbed directly into the bloodstream.
Normal flora of the cecum:
Protozoa and *anaerobic* bacteria—*Bacteroides sp, Streptococcus fecalis,* and *Clostridium spp* (some strains are harmful).

7. Colon. Contractions of the *haustrae* in the proximal colon separate small particles, sending them backward into the cecum. Larger particles are eliminated as hard droppings, or *fecal pellets.* Vitamin-rich cecal material is formed into soft droppings or *cecotropes* .

8. Fusus coli between the proximal and *distal* colon regulates the excretion of hard and soft droppings.

9. Anus. Cecotropes, packaged in mucus-membrane clusters, are consumed directly and returned to the digestive system.

10. Reingested cecotropes. Protected in mucus-membrane packages, cecotropes continue to ferment in the stomach for several hours, until they pass to the small intestine where the nutrients are absorbed. (Cheeke 1987)

VETERINARY CONSULTANTS:
Carolynn Harvey, D.V.M.,
Karl Waidhofer, D.V.M.,
Richard Evans, D.V.M., MS

ADDITIONAL REFERENCES:
McLaughlin, C.A. and R.B. Chaisson, 1990. Pp 59-64 in *Laboratory Anatomy of the Rabbit.* William C. Brown. Percy, D.H. and S.W. Barthold. 1993. Pp 179-80 in *Pathology of Laboratory Rodents and Rabbits.* Iowa State University Press.

PATH OF UNFERMENTED MATERIAL (FOOD, FECES)
PATH OF FERMENTED MATERIAL (CECOTROPES)

Esophagus

Pyloric valve (small intestine begins)

Liver

Duodenum
Pancreas

Stomach

Reingested cecotropes continue to ferment

Small Intestine

Jejunum

Large fiber is separated forming fecal pellets

Appendix

Proximal Colon   Haustrae

Illeoceco-colonic junction

Colon contractions move small particles and fluid back into the cecum

Ileum

Excretion of cecotropes and fecal pellets are regulated at the fusus coli

Cecum

Fermenting cecal material

Fecal pellets pass through the colon and rectum and are eliminated.

Distal Colon

Rectum

Cecotropes, excreted as a mucus membrane surrounded cluster, are reingested

Anus

DIAGRAM: BOB HARRIMAN

Digestive Disruption

ASIDE FROM BEING an amazing mechanism, the digestive system in a rabbit must operate at full capacity to maintain good health. When any part of the GI (gastrointestinal) tract shuts down, the result can be life threatening.

PROBLEMS IN THE STOMACH AND DUODENUM

Dietary fiber keeps things moving. Without it, swallowed hair or synthetics from your home furnishings, along with pelleted feed, can block bunny's digestive flow.

Stomach impactions. We are reminded by Dr. Susan Brown to look for the causes rather than effect. "The primary problem is not an accumulation of hair in the stomach but rather a problem with sluggish motility of the gastrointestinal tract, leading to dehydration and impaction..." (Brown 01).

If motility problems are left uncorrected, the impaction may remain in the stomach and increase in size, while bunny's appetite decreases. Sometimes smaller wads of undigested material, stuck together with bits of fur, can get through the stomach and lodge in a narrow passage in the small intestine, usually at the duodenum. The resulting obstruction stops the flow from the stomach.

Most motility problems can be prevented by dietary fiber, but sometimes rabbits don't consume the necessary fiber because of stress, dental disorders, or other diseases, so it's important to get to the "root" of the problem. Obstructions may also be caused by congenital deformations, adhesions, lesions, or inflammations—anything that will make passage difficult through the GI tract.

FIGURE 2: Gastric and duodenal Impactions

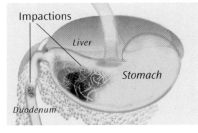

A large impaction may continue to increase in size within the stomach, until it forms a blockage. A small impaction can form a blockage, when/if it lodges in a narrow passage in the small intestine.

Trichobezoars. True hairballs usually take longer to form than impactions and are seldom seen in our house rabbits. They are more common in laboratory rabbits who are caged and bored for prolonged periods of time without exercise. Although boredom and lack of roughage are not normally present in our companion rabbits' lives, we can't prevent all motility-slowing stresses. After the loss of a partner, some rabbits become obsessive fur chewers, but decrease their hay eating, and wind up with large quantities of hair that they are unable to pass. Rabbits don't rid themselves of swallowed hair by vomiting.

Bloat is a serious condition that may develop secondary to impaction anywhere in the digestive tract. Gas can form directly behind a blockage, or in any area where motility has slowed down, extending the stomach or the part of the intestine affected. Bloat can cause severe discomfort, shock, and death if not treated.

If your bunny has a tight abdomen, is in obvious pain, (not interested in his favorite treat), rush him to the vet. In many cases, bloat occurs in the stomach itself, and immediate relief can be achieved with a gastric tube to remove gas, pain medication, and intravenous fluids to rehydrate and soften the impaction. X-rays are often useful in showing gas formations and indicating more specifically where the problem is.

If the stomach continues to bloat after several attempts at decompression, there is little choice left. Surgery is the last resort and is only used when less invasive procedures have failed.

DIAGRAM: BOB HARRIMAN

"Prevention of both hairballs and impactions is largely dietary."

PROBLEMS IN THE CECUM AND ILEUS

A rabbit relies on anaerobic bacteria (grow without oxygen) in the cecum to break down cellulose. If the microbial balance of the cecum is altered by moldy food, or by an overload of sugar or starch, this can cause an overgrowth of harmful bacteria that can make your bunny sick. And not only that—if these harmful bacteria continue to grow, they can produce deadly toxins that will kill your rabbit (enterotoxemia). That's why it was stated in the previous chapter, that high starch and sugary treats, or moldy food, should not be part of your rabbit's diet.

This is also why your veterinarian can prescribe only certain drugs for your rabbit. They must work on the illness without destroying the intestinal bacteria necessary for digestion.

Enteritis (inflammation of the small intestine) can occur in rabbits when the cecum has slowed down enough to alter the gut flora. This affects the area of the small intestine (the ileum) next to the cecum. The intestinal lining produces a mucus coating over the inflamed area.

Cecal impaction occurs when the cecum receives too much low-fiber food and spends one to four days (sometimes longer) fermenting the material. A portion of the cecal contents is emptied daily, but not all. If more small material enters the cecum than exits, the result may be altered gut flora or a cecal impaction.

The cecum empties at a slower rate when dietary fiber drops below 14%. Scientific studies have shown that large particles (5mm), in marked feed can pass through a rabbit's digestive tract in as few as 5 hours. (Sakaguchi 1992). Give your rabbit plenty of coarse indigestible organic material to keep the gut working at an optimum rate.

Dehydration is another cause of cecal impaction. This may be due to hot weather, insufficient water intake, ingestion of water-absorbing fiber (such as psyllium used in human laxatives) or large quantities of absorbent litterbox material. When fluids are needed elsewhere, they are drawn from the cecum's reservoir into the blood, leaving a hard accumulating mass in the cecum.

HOSPITAL AND HOME CARE

All of the above conditions are serious enough to mandate prompt veterinary attention and specific treatment. Additionally, drugs, such as Metoclopramide or Cisapride, that stimulate intestinal motility, might be given, but not when an actual blockage is determined (may build up too much pressure behind the blockage). Anti inflammatory drugs might be used if inflammation is involved.

Your bunny will most likely be treated and monitored in the hospital, succeeded by a home program that you will provide. The basic home program for motility problems is as follows:

Fluids. These are often given subcutaneously (under the skin), usually twice a day.

Pain medication, if prescribed for gas discomfort.

Hay. Any kind he/she will eat—to increase motility.

Fresh produce, especially leafy greens—offered several times a day.

Encourage fiber intake by your anorectic bunny with constant fresh offerings.

Once your bunny's appetite has recovered, it should be watched carefully. Anorexia is both a sign of illness and a cause of further illness by slowing down GI motility all the more.

Routines help you monitor your bunny's appetite. Make it a routine to give give your bunny a fresh offering of his preferred veggies three times a day. Note how enthusiastic he is first thing in the morning, then again after you get home from work, then just before you go to bed. At-home observations are invaluable for catching illness early. ■

Microbial Infection

ANYONE WHO HAS TREATED a persistent infection in a rabbit would believe that rabbits have a hard time dealing with infections. There are several ways in which rabbits come down with infectious disease. They can be exposed to pathogens (harmful microbes) in the environment that gain entry through inhalation into the respiratory tract or ascendance up the urinary tract. More often, rabbits can become infected by opportunistic bacteria already residing within their GI tract or on their skin surfaces. These bacteria do not normally present a problem unless they are introduced to sterile areas of the body (i.e. blood, subcutaneous tissue). This happens when the physical barriers (skin/membrane) are penetrated by a puncture or a bite wound, allowing entry of surface bacteria.

Infectious agents can cause disease in a number of ways. Some are not particularly virulent but can colonize well and result in a persistent infection that the host has difficulty clearing. This often results in inflammation and tissue damage. On the other end of the spectrum, there are pathogens which secrete very potent toxins, so only a low level of infection produces serious consequences. Viral pathogens can replicate very quickly in a host organism, resulting in extensive cell lysis and tissue damage. It should be noted that in some cases the immune response that is induced by the infection is as damaging as the infection itself.

DEFENSES

An animal's immune system defends against invading microorganisms by producing antibodies that destroy them. When the animal is stressed, physically or psychologically, the immune system may be weakened enough that opportunistic pathogens can get a foothold.

Bacterial colonization may remain in the local area, or it may become septicemic and spread via the blood from a less critical location to a vital organ. Sometimes the infection may become walled off, into an abscess, where it can't be "seen" and destroyed by the immune system and where antibiotics can't penetrate. An abscess may eventually rupture and spill its contents into surrounding tissue and then become septicemic. Bacteria, even from a walled-off infection, may slip through small sinuses to form adjacent pockets.

CULTURING

Samples of tissue or pus from an infected area can be sent by your vet to a laboratory for identification of the infecting agents and a list of the drugs they are sensitive to. Your veterinarian uses this information in prescribing the appropriate drug.

In the table below, the HRS Rabbit Health Database shows bacteria, cultured from 31 different rabbits with disease symptoms. In some cases,

Table 9.1: *Cultures from 31 diseased rabbits*

Organism (genus)	Tissue/Pus: internal organ	pus: external abscess	eye/nasal discharge	Urine	Total
Staphylococcus	1	13	3	3	20
Proteus	1	8	1	8	18
Pasteurella	2	5	6	2	15
Streptococcus	4	1	5	3	13
No growth	1	3	3	4	11
Pseudomonas	3		4	1	8
Enterococcus	3	1	1		5
Acinetobacter	1		1	1	3
Actinomyces	1	2			3
Bacteroides		3			3
Corynebacterium	1		1	1	3
Aspergillus (fungus)	2				2
Bordetella			2		2

as many as three different cultures were grown from a single rabbit (retests are not included). Individual reports list species and groups, as well as sensitivity and resistance to antibiotics.

Other bacteria cultured once each were: Acromobacter, Actinobaccillus, Actinobacter, Aeromonas, Clostridia, Enterobacter, Escherichia, Fusobacterium, Klebsiella, Moraxella, Neisseira, and Rhodococcus.

Pathogens causing diseases in rabbits are not always possible to culture. An alternative test is the ELISA (enzyme linked immunosorbant assay) which tests the immune response to a particular organism. This can be done for detecting Pasteurella as well as pathogens causing the following diseases in rabbits:

Encephalitozoonosis: Infection by sporozoan parasite, Encephalitozoon cuniculi. Some rabbits never show clinical signs of the disease (neurological disorders and some types of kidney disease). Other rabbits are severely affected by it. It's possible that the long term challenge to the immune system by E.cuniculi may leave the rabbit more susceptible to other diseases.

Tyzzer's disease: Infection by the bacterium, Clostridium piliformis. This may cause immediate illness —bloat/diarrhea/enteritis— and even death or may damage internal organs (liver, heart, intestine) leaving them predisposed to other diseases. Sometimes no disease is seen at all.

The following information is from the HRS Rabbit Health Database, which is compiled from veterinary records that have been mailed to our headquarters. Over 500 tests were done over a ten year period. Many of the seropositive rabbits have been followed through their lifetime. Obviously, we have learned that while many rabbits are infected, not all develop disease.

Table 9.2. *Ratio of disease symptoms to seropositive rabbits*

ELISA TEST	SEROPOSITIVE RABBITS	DEVELOPED SYMPTOMS	NECROPSIES DONE	POST MORTEM EVIDENCE FOUND
E.cuniculi	175	52	41	21
C.piliformis	101	9	27	19

Exposure to the above pathogens can be reduced by frequent changing of litterboxes that are used by multiple animals. Do it away from the rabbit living area, since the spores can become airborne. If your rabbits have outdoor playpens, keep them securely shut, even when your bunnies aren't in them. We don't want the local wildlife to contaminate the bunnies' pens.

DRUG THERAPY

Antibiotics function as either a bacteriostatic, which stop the growth of multiplying bacteria, or as a bactedicidal, which stop metabolism within the bacterial cell and kills it. Both are used for rabbits. The goal in antibiotic treatment is to buy time until the immune system can take over the job of destroying the infection. In rabbits, this can take several weeks, or even several months, especially when the infections are in the more difficult to reach areas, such as bony tissue, the nasal cavity, the brain, inner ear, lymph nodes or any internal organ. These must be treated with a hardworking systemic antibiotic.

Many drugs are available to help your bunny fight disease. Veterinarians have become increasingly educated and know which ones to use for what. They exchange information online, and everybody stays up to date. Warnings about drugs dangerous to rabbits, such as Amoxicillin, are no longer necessary. Drugs to use and not use for rabbits have changed somewhat in the past ten years. The list on the following page is used at the veterinary hospital in my area.   ■

Rabbit Formulary
By CAROLYNN HARVEY, D.V.M.

ANTIBIOTICS

Amikacin – 15 mg/kg SQ SID.

Amoxicillin: DO NOT USE.

Azithromycin (Zithromax): 20-30 mg/kg q24h initially, then 2x/week, or prn for maintenance. Watch for GI upset.

Cephalosporins: DO NOT USE.

Chloramphenicol:20–50 mg/kg BID PO (have specially formulated) 20 mg/kg SQ BID (stings, may need to dilute) *Minimize your exposure. Wear gloves. Wash your hands after handling, and keep out of reach of children.*

Ciprofloxacin:10- 20 mg/kg PO SID.

Enrofloxacin (Baytril): 5–10 mg/kg PO or SQ BID (or 10- 20mg/kg SID – may see GI upset at 20 mg/kg) can give IV, but give slowly and watch for histamine release.

Pen G, Benzathine/Procaine: 20,000:30,000 u/# SubQ every other day for 2-6 weeks, then same dose 2x/week. *Watch for GI upset, which can be fatal. In repeat uses, watch for anaphylaxis (consider dispensing epinephrine for emergency use).*

Pen G, Procaine: 20,000–30,000 u/# (0.05-0.1 cc/#) SQ daily for short periods, or once a week (recommended by VIN).

Metronidazole: 10mg/kg PO BID.

Tetracycline (Panmycin Aquadrops): 10mg/# PO BID. *Watch for kidney failure if used with other kidney-impacting drugs like Baytril.*

Trimethoprim-Sulfa: 30 mg/kg PO BID.

NSAIDS, ANALGESICS

Aspirin: 40–80 mg/kg PO BID (empirical dose); 100mg/kg BID published dose.

Buprenorphine: 0.005– 0.01 mg/kg SQ, IM or in mouth. *Note that this is lower than the published dose, which seems too sedating . Is more effective when absorbed by the mouth than when swallowed.*

Butorphanol (Torbugesic): 0.25 mg/kg /SQ, IM, IV. Can be used orally, but short half life.

Carprofen: 10mg/# PO BID. Conservative dose, can probably safely double. *Watch for azotemia, rare "sedated" reaction.*

EMLA Cream: Shave area, apply cream, wait 5 minutes for superficial numbing. Wear gloves to apply.

Flunixin Meglumine (Banamine): 1 mg/kg SQ or IV.

Ibuprofen: 7.5-20 mg/kg BID to TID PO. (e.g. Children's Motrin: 20 mg ibuprofen/cc) *Watch for GI upset, typhlitis.*

Ketoprofen: 1 mg/kg SQ

Meloxicam: 0.2-0.5 mg/kg PO SID-BID. *Dr Harvey's starting dose is 0.2 mg/kg BID. HRS fosterers report that it doesn't seem to last 24 hours at 0.1 mg/kg for postop pain.*

GI DRUGS

Cholestyramine: 2 gm/average size rabbit (for most brands, about 1 tsp) given as a slurry PO SID.

Cisapride: 2.5–5 mg per rabbit PO TID. *This is no longer on the market and needs to be obtained through a compounding pharmacy.*

Metoclopramide (Reglan): 0.2-0.5 mg/kg PO, SQ, IV TID.

Sucralfate: 125 : 250 mg per rabbit TID as slurry.

Sulfadimethoxine (Albon): 25 mg/kg PO SID x 14 days, or until fecal is negative.

PARASITICIDES

Albendazole: 7-20 mg/kg SID x 3-6 months for E. cuniculi.

Carbaryl powder: 2x per week.

Fenbendazole (Panacur): 20 mg/kg SID x 21 days for E. cuniculi.

Fipronil (Frontline): DO NOT USE. *Seizures and death reported.*

Imidacloprid (Advantage): Use cat dose.

Ivermectin 1% (Ivomec): 300mcg/kg PO or SQ every 7-14 days.

Lufenuron (Program): Use cat dose.

Lime-Sulfur Dip (Lym Dip): Every one to two weeks. *Dipping/bathing process itself can cause shock or collapse.*

Oxibendazole: 20mg/kg SID x 3-6 months for E. cuniculi.

Selamectin (Revolution): 6-12 mg/kg monthly (15 mg for rabbit under 4#, 30 mg for rabbits over 4#).

Dr. Carolynn Harvey practices veterinary medicine at VCA Bay Area Pet Hospital in Oakland California. She is also Health Director of the National House Rabbit Society.

Bunny's Veterinary Exam

THE NEXT PRIORITY to knowing what is normal for your rabbit is knowing when to get the professional help of a good rabbit doctor. One of the most important alliances you will ever form to ensure your rabbit's longevity is with your veterinarian. You must be able to work together on bunny's health care program.

Make the first appointment early. Start your bunny with a head-to-toe exam in your veterinarian's office and get a file set up. Then you will be ready if an emergency arises. Your veterinarian will check for respiratory disease, listen to heart and digestive sounds, and palpate the abdomen to check for organ or intestinal abnormalities.

During the palpation, the veterinarian will also check for lumps and bumps that may indicate malignancy. Cancer is very common in unspayed females, especially after their fifth year. It's best to have spay or neuter surgery done well before then.

Of course, you want the sex determined—something not so easy to do if your bunny is extremely young, because the genitals of immature males and females look similar. Unless you adopt an already neutered/spayed rabbit, one of the first exams should be a "pre-operative."

Depending on your rabbit's age and health conditions, your veterinarian may recommend a blood panel to check for anemia, kidney function, and liver enzymes. This will help indicate any special precautions that need to be taken prior to or during surgery. ■

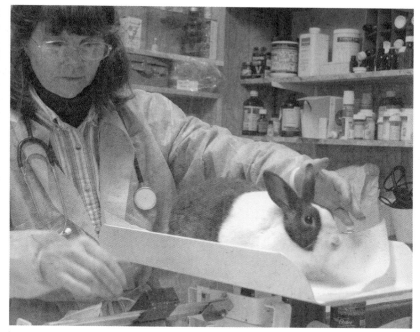

Exam basics include a weight check for gains and losses between exams.

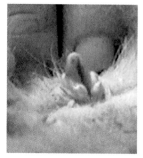

Female: *The vulva can be seen when pressure is applied above the genital area. The protrusion is pointed.*

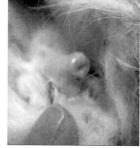

Male: *The penis is also seen by applying pressure above genitals. The protrusion is round and flat at the end.*

Elective Surgery

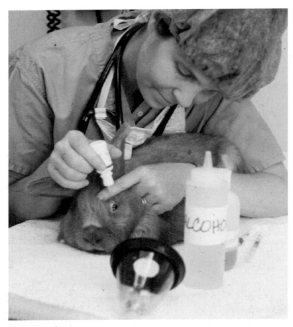

A surgery patient is calmed and her eyes are treated, prior to other preparations before she goes under the anesthesia.

WHEN SURGERY IS REQUIRED to remove an infection, a tumor, a hairball, or a bladder stone, you have no choice but to proceed in order to improve your bunny's chance for survival. On the other hand, spaying or neutering is considered elective surgery, primarily intended to improve behavior and ensure good toilet habits, in addition to preventing pregnancies. There are also health benefits, such as fewer infections due to bites and scratches and less inclination to urinary infections. And a complete spay, of course, eliminates the risk of uterine cancer (up to 80% in 5-year olds).

Rabbit surgery has become much safer in recent years as veterinarians perform them routinely. Neutering helps both health and behavior. Males can be neutered as soon as the testicles have descended. This can happen any time after 3ž months. Females are usually spayed at 6-8 months old, depending on size.

House Rabbit Society chapters all over the country have had many thousands of rabbits spayed or neutered prior to putting them up for adoption. Our rabbits are not fasted, but they are not fed immediately before surgery. This is to keep them from having left over food in their mouth when they go under anesthesia (danger of aspiration). They are offered food as soon as they awaken.

ANESTHESIA

Most veterinary hospitals are now equipped with isoflurane, which is the anesthesia of choice for rabbits. Safety of the procedure, however, does not rest entirely with the anesthesia but with the skill of the practitioner. The isoflurane deaths that were reported to us many years ago, were mostly due to lack of pre-anesthesias, adequate preparations, and possibly waking too quickly. Veterinarians now have experience using isoflurane.

Other types of anesthesias can also be used safely on rabbits. Halothane is used in many low-cost neuter clinics. High volume clinics usually acquire such enormous experience that they can use halothane safely. Pre-anesthesias are particularly important, since a combination of adrenaline and halothane can be lethal. If you have an exceptionally high-strung nervous rabbit, be sure to let the surgeon know so that bunny can be well sedated with pre-anesthetic before the gas is given.

While rabbit surgeries may be safer if done before 1 year old, we don't always have always have that age choice. Many of our rescued rabbits are 5-6-years old at the time of surgery and their recovery is excellent.   ■

Conditions Requiring Treatment

Because RABBITS have not lived in human homes as long as dogs and cats, there is less common knowledge about when rabbits' lives are in danger, how serious a problem is, and when to get immediate veterinary care. Taking a wait-and-see attitude can be fatal for a rabbit. Here are a few conditions that might require a judgment call.

Animal attacks. If your rabbit has been attacked by a dog, raccoon, or any predatory animal, take him to the vet, even if you see no bite wounds. These are sometimes unobservable without a veterinary exam. Also, a bunny might experience shock that may not be apparent for several hours. Precautionary treatment for shock is advisable anytime a rabbit has been subjected to the trauma of an attack.

Bleeding toenails. When toenails grow too long, they can break off and bleed. This may not require rushing off to the vet, but it does require adequate cleaning with a disinfectant. You may have to apply a styptic powder to stop the bleeding. Keep bunny confined on a clean surface until the bleeding has stopped. If bone is exposed, antibiotics might be necessary to prevent infection, so a veterinary exam is needed. For clipping, see page 86)

Broken bones. While many fractures show immediate symptoms (e.g., dragging one foot), others may not be so obvious. If the rabbit has suffered trauma and/or is favoring one limb, X-rays are needed to determine the extent of the injury.

Conjunctivitis. Runny eyes are not uncommon in rabbits. Many rabbits with runny eyes show no other signs of illness. There are a variety of causes including allergies or long term low pathogenic infection. External irritants may be involved, such as ammonia. Some Rabbits may not have well developed tear ducts.

Culturing for bacterial infection is sometimes difficult, so we normally treat topically, in case there is one. Your veterinarian may choose to flush the tear ducts with saline solution and prescribe an ophthalmic ointment or drops for you to apply at home. If the apparent infection extends to other areas, your vet will undoubtedly start your bunny on systemic antibiotics as well as topical.

Cuts and lacerations. Rabbits become infected quite easily and have a hard time dealing with infections. Always have a bottle of wound disinfectant (polyhydroxydine or chlorhexidine solution) on hand and use it immediately, if bunny incurs a scratch. Follow up with triple-antibiotic ointment. Keep any cut, scratch, laceration, or open wound clean and check it daily for several days.

Topical eye drops.
Perry's runny eyes are treated twice daily with ophthalmic solution.

Deep cuts, punctures, or large wounds should be seen by the veterinarian. Stitches and systemic antibiotics may be necessary.

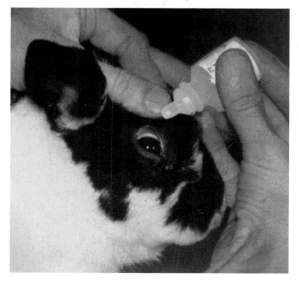

Diarrhea, constipation, no stools. Diagnostic testing is needed to determine the cause. Accompanying behavior will help determine how urgently veterinary care is needed. If bunny has diarrhea and is listless, rush him to the hospital. If he is constipated, bloated (tight belly), and sitting in a scrunched up position, put your ear to his abdomen and listen. Too much gut sound or no gut sounds at all are danger signals. Don't delay in calling your vet with these details. Your bunny will most likely need a same-day appointment for an exam.

Ear mites. Noticeable signs are head and ear shaking. Inspection of the ear reveals dark scabby material inside it. While it's possible to work liquid medication down into heavily infested ears, this can be extremely painful. Systemic treatments, such as ivermectin and selamectin, are much more comfortable for the bunny. One dose of oral/injectable ivermectin is followed by a second a week later. Topical selamectin is used once a month or as needed. Both eliminate mites. Recheck often. They may still be present in the environment.

Checking evidence: Dr. Susan Brown of the Midwest Bird and Exotic Animal Hospital, Chicago, examines ears for signs of mites or other abnormalities.

Flea infestation. Control of fleas is normally a matter of upkeep. Flea infestation becomes a disease state when it is severe, and masses of black grains of dirt (actually dried blood) are seen on the skin. Fleas can cause skin allergies in many animals, and prolonged severe flea infestation in some rabbits can result in loss of blood to the extent of causing anemia. This occurs especially among older less agile animals who are not able to groom themselves.

Phoebe's itchy spine is checked for fleas. Flaky dandruff and hair loss can mean fur mites or flea allergy. You may not see fleas, but "flea dirt" tells you that they have dined on your bunny.

Severe flea infestations should be attacked aggressively—but this does not include a flea dip. For an already compromised animal, a dip can be fatal. And flea collars are lethal for rabbits who manage to chew them. Traditional (carbaryl) flea powders can be used, or you may prefer one of the newer systemic treatments, such as selamectin, that are applied to a small area on the back of the neck. Products with imidacloprid or lufenuron have been safely used on rabbits. *Do not use products containing fipronil.*

Fly strike. Compromised animals are more vulnerable, but any rabbit with open wounds or a dirty bottom, may fall victim to egg-laying flies. Maggots not only cause damage by burrowing into flesh,

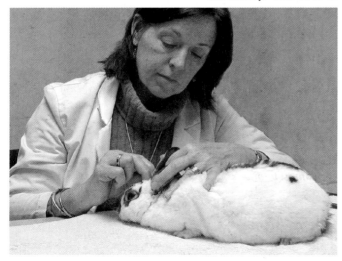

PHOTOS: LEFT, RICHARD NYE; RIGHT, MARINELL HARRIMAN

but they also release toxins that can cause death.

If you find a fly-stricken rabbit, take immediate action. If you are within 10 minutes of your veterinarian, go immediately. If not, you can plunge the stricken area under running tap water and wash the larvae off yourself. You must still hurry to vet. There may be more larvae or eggs that you have not detected, and your veterinarian will want to give fluids that will detoxify your stricken bunny and treat for shock.

The absolute best way to deal with fly strike is prevention. Susceptible bunnies should be kept indoors, with good screens on doors and windows. If you can't keep flies off your bunny you can prevent their damage by combing the eggs out of the fur. Be sure to comb legs and feet as well the spinal area.

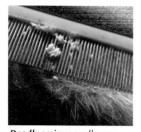

Deadly serious are fly eggs. These can stick like little burrs in the coat, but a daily combing can get rid of them before they hatch.

Fur mites (cheyletiella). Evidence is seen, especially on the lower spine, where a thick layer of itchy flaky skin has developed. Often the clumps of hair will fall out along with the flakes of skin. Both flea allergies and fur mites cause these uncomfortable skin conditions. Both can be treated with flea powders. Again, use carbaryl powder (pyrethrins may cause respiratory problems. Fur mites, like ear mites, can also be treated ivermectin or selamectin.

Head tilt. The cause is usually a bacterial infection in the inner ear that affects the rabbit's balance. Other causes might be parasitic disease in the brain or stroke. A veterinary evaluation and prescriptive treatment are needed.

Heat stress. It's too hot even in your house. Bunny is panting and has a wet nose. During hot weather, your freezer should have milk or juice cartons full of ice to lay next to your bunny on hot days. Misting the ears with

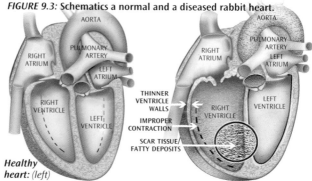

FIGURE 9.3: Schematics a normal and a diseased rabbit heart.

Healthy heart: (left) shows normal muscle contractions. ***Diseased heart*** *(right) shows example of "flabby" heart muscle, which does not contract properly; has thinner ventricle walls; may have scar tissue, or fatty deposits.*

cool water can bring the temperature down. A wet towel hung across one end of the cage or run, with plenty of air blowing through, makes an evaporative cooler.

Heart disease. This may not be obvious and may be hidden behind other (possibly secondary) diseases. Bouts of enteritis are sometimes secondary to poor circulation caused by cardiovascular disease. We have learned that heart disease may develop as a result of damage to the heart muscle, possibly due to infections. Cardiomyopathy can mimic or even cause other problems. Signs may be "incoordination, weakness, weight loss, depression, enteritis, difficult breathing." (Deeb 01)

Usually a series of tests are needed before your veterinarian can diagnose heart disease and prescribe medication.

Lumps, bumps. You needn't rush to the hospital in the middle of the night if you notice a lump on your normal-acting bunny. You should, however, make an appointment and have it checked fairly soon. Abscesses and tumors can be serious, and treatment depends on specifically what it is.

PHOTO: MARINELL HARRIMAN; HEART DIAGRAM: BOB HARRIMAN

Malocclusion. Whether due to hereditary factors or to injuries that pull the teeth out of alignment, some rabbits develop a malocclusion. This means that the teeth do not line up. They overgrow, and bunny can't eat.

Veterinarians have become experienced at treating this problem, so if you have a rabbit with maloccluded incisors or molars, it is best to discuss your options with your veterinarian and work out a teeth-trimming program that works for you or even removal of the incisors. The condition does need to be treated, or it can result in root and jaw infections, which are very difficult to reach with antibiotics.

Keep on smiling. Teeth can be checked from the underside or from the "knee" position (on page 80). Mainly you are checking for teeth that don't line up, as well as other abnormalities.

Paralysis. Partial or complete paralysis can have many diverse causes. Besides trauma to the head or back, causes may include strokes; tumors; bacterial infections; protozoan infections; viruses; nematodes; toxins; degenerative disease; intervertebral disc disease; and even osteoporosis. A common cause of rabbit paralysis is encephalitozoonosis (page 69).

Rabbits who experience loss of mobility should have a complete neurological exam and blood workup. Treatment and care depends on severity and specific cause. For long-term care for paralysis see page 82.

Raccoon roundworm (Baylisascaris). Eggs are deposited in soil and vegetation where raccoons defecate and may be ingested by grazing animals. Since rabbits are not the target host, the larvae migrate to neural tissue causing nearly 100% mortality. No treatment is recognized, however some anecdotal success with parasiticides have been reported.

Prevention is imperative. Keep all feed and hay securely stored, and keep bunny off the ground where raccoons have roamed.

Red urine. A urinalysis is needed to determine if this is caused by blood in the urine. If blood is present, it may indicate infection, urinary stones, or possibly cancer. Otherwise the reddening of the urine color may be due simply to dietary or weather changes.

Respiratory disease. Noticeable symptoms are nose discharge or sneezing. There may also be rattly or labored breathing. Labored breathing in a rabbit is not short panting but rather long hard breaths.

Some rabbits may be experiencing allergic reactions to bedding material or simply to dust. The same symptoms may indicate a long-term chronic condition or the onset of a life-threatening disease.

Upper respiratory disease may be caused by infection or obstruction of the upper airways (nasal passages, sinuses, pharynx). Lower respiratory (lung) disease can be quite serious and may be caused by infection or tumors, or it might be secondary to heart disease. All respiratory diseases should be evaluated by a veterinarian to determine the course of treatment.

Seizures, coma, stupor. Any time you find your rabbit unconscious for any reason it is a medical emergency, and you need to rush your rabbit to the doctor. The cause may be electrocution, poisoning or a range of other possibilities. If you suspect poisoning, take the substance in question along with you.

Sore hocks, foot abscesses. This is a perplexing problem for many rabbits, after fur on the feet has worn down, exposing the skin and forming calluses. Sores occur when calluses are constantly exposed to wet surfaces in resting areas or litterboxes. Keep the litterbox changed daily or topped with dry material so that the surface next to the feet is always dry.

Moisture-damaged skin is easily cracked, allowing dirt to penetrate. Dirt in an open foot wound nearly always causes difficult-to-treat infection. Disinfect all open wounds with polyhydrox-ydine or chlorhexidine solution. If any swelling occurs, take bunny to the veterinarian. Antibiotics, bandages, and long-term treatment may be necessary.

Straining. Symptoms of urinary problems may be first noticed in abnormal litterbox-posturing and sometimes squealing. A series of little puddles around the litterbox, instead of in it, and excessive

Slew-footed Luke is predisposed to callused heels due to improperly healed broken legs. Padding his feet with Vet-wrap combined with the blanket ground-cover prevents excessive callus buildup.

water drinking might be signs of urinary disorders. Any of these symptoms warrant a veterinary exam.

Kidney/bladder stones and "sludge" urine are fairly common in rabbits. The causes are complex. Infection, high calcium/vitamin D intake, and low fluid intake may all contribute. However, these "causes" may be the side effect of something else. Since urinary infection is often involved, treatment usually includes antibiotics.

Thymoma. This is a "benign" tumor that arises from the thymus gland and grows. While not a cancerous growth that metastasizes, it eventually causes death by squeezing the space in the chest cavity. Your veterinarian will monitor the growth. If the growth is very slow, your bunny may have a normal life expectancy. If the growth is rapid, your veterinarian may try to find a surgical expert who can remove the thymoma or explore radiation therapy, which has caused remission in several cases.

Urine scald. This may be an indication of urinary disease but more often is a secondary problem in crippled, sick, or arthritic rabbits who urinate on themselves. Skin constantly exposed to irritating urine becomes inflamed.

To treat it, clip the hair away to eliminate wicking by the hair, then rinse off all urine with warm water (see pages 82, 83, and 87). Apply anti-inflammatory powder or cream.

Wet cheeks due to chronically runny eyes. Wet fur on the cheeks under runny eyes may cause irritation to the skin and consequent loss of hair. Mild wetness can be blotted with tissue. Very wet and matted fur on the cheeks can be cleansed with ophthalmic saline solution and blotted, then flea combed for remaining debris.

DIAGNOSTIC TOOLS

Fortunately, there are many diagnostic tools available to your veterinarian. Heart disease can sometimes be detected by radiographs but more definitively with ultrasound. Ultrasound is most useful at revealing heart, liver, kidney disease, and sometimes cysts or abscesses within the thorax. MRI or CT scans are good for looking at bone and internal tissues and provide detailed radiographic pictures.

ECGs can be done to assess heart problems, and lab work, such as cultures, blood chemistries, and urinalysis are valuable in making a diagnosis. ∎

Power of the Psyche

SOMETHING VERY SELDOM mentioned in veterinary manuals but acknowledged by experienced rabbit veterinarians is the importance of dealing with the rabbit psyche. Generally, this is thought to be accommodated in the veterinarian's "bedside manner"—soothing and sweet talking the rabbit into calmness.

In caring for quite a few sanctuary rabbits with long and short-term illnesses, we have seen some miracles of motivation. We are convinced that friendship therapy contributes to the recovery or at least the stabilization of sick rabbits.

MIND OVER MATTER

We had a peculiar case with our 8-year-old Jefty. His depression over losing his mate to cancer triggered abnormal fur chewing. A good part of his body was suddenly bald, and a veterinary exam revealed that most of that hair was in his stomach. It seemed very unlikely that the huge mass would ever break up and pass. We started him on the "hairball" remedies and tried to stabilize him enough to survive surgery. Meanwhile, I added one more remedy to the treatment. I introduced him to 10-year-old Sieglinda, who had recently lost her partner.

We postponed the surgery a few more days since the pair was bonding so well, and we wanted to give Jefty all the morale boosters he could get before the risky surgery. By the end of those few days, his improvement was so remarkable that we decided to wait and see. The fur mass was still in his stomach, but it was getting smaller.

He now had a reason to eat the hay and greens in front of him. He had someone to dine with and to share his pineapple cocktails with. In the next few weeks, this bald anorectic "skeleton" of a rabbit regained his handsome figure. .

A strong argument for looking at the psychological as well as the physical animal is that, yes,

Friendship therapy: Assisting the antibiotics, Octavia is credited for saving Phoebe's life, after pulling her through a 2-day crisis with pneumonia.

physical things must take place in the cure, but a mental incentive can sometimes be the button that sets those physical things in motion.

FOR PRACTICAL PURPOSES

Of course we don't introduce contagiously- sick rabbits into a new group, but separating bonded rabbits, after they become ill, does more harm than good. If your rabbit is struggling for life and a cherished companion is nearby, the last thing you want to do is separate them. I keep bonded pairs together even when the sick rabbit must be hospitalized.

This is *routine* in Dr. Carolynn Harvey's practice, and we urge veterinarians everywhere to follow this wonderful example. The entire hospital staff knows that whenever a House Rabbit Society member checks in a critically ill rabbit who is one of a bonded pair, a second rabbit will be checked in for moral support. That's just part of the treatment.

Credit for our rabbits' survival must be given to excellent veterinary care, but the psyche factor is an additional tool in the doctor's bag of tricks and it may at times mean the difference between life and death. ∎

Home Health Routines

Programs to ensure the best possible health for your bunny's various life stages may involve preventive care, convalescent care, chronic care, and sometimes long-term care.

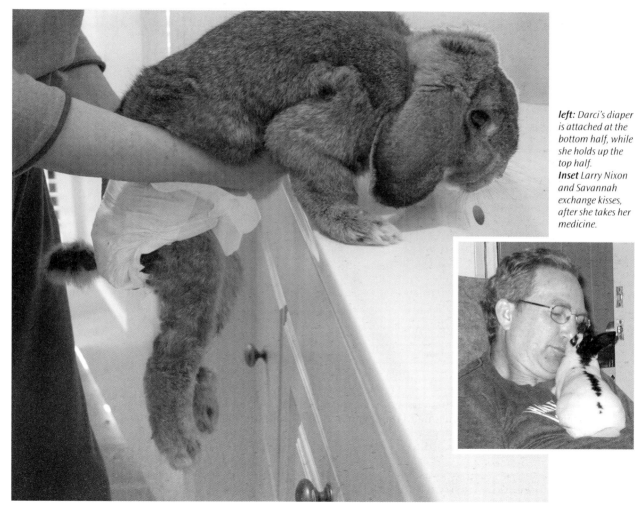

left: Darci's diaper is attached at the bottom half, while she holds up the top half.
Inset *Larry Nixon and Savannah exchange kisses, after she takes her medicine.*

PHOTOS: ABOVE, TANIA HARRIMAN; INSET, JUDITH PIERCE

Convalescent Care

W HEN YOUR BUNNY COMES HOME to convalesce from surgery or a serious illness or injury after a hospital stay, recovery is expected. Your job is to provide the support and home care that your veterinarian prescribes.

Your bunny should be confined for a few days after spay/neuter surgery to prevent overdoing: two days for males; about five or six days for females. Mixed sexes should be separated for about two weeks, in case of stored sperm.

Confinement can be in a clean disinfected cage or a small covered pen. Provide comfortable bedding so that there will be no inclination to sleep in the litterbox (and contaminate the suture area). Confinement may be even more restrictive and for a much longer period for a bunny convalescing from fractures or back injuries. Keep the bunny comfortable with padding and rotate his toys and position.

Most bunnies are able to eat immediately after surgery, but some may be anorexic for a couple of days. Offer hay at this time to get the digestive system working again. If your veterinarian advises supplemental feeding during convalescence, you can use a prepared formula (Critical Care from Oxbow Hay) or blend your own (page 59).

GIVING MEDICINE

When your bunny comes home from the hospital, he will most likely have medication and treatment prescribed. If injections or subcutaneous fluids are necessary, your veterinarian will show you how to administer them. In some cases, a convalescing rabbit needs subcutaneous fluids, not only to keep up hydration but to balance electrolytes and help flush out toxins. Lactated Ringer's Solution (LRS) is given for a number of conditions including: toxicity, kidney malfunction, fever, and digestive upsets. B-vitamins can be added to the bag of LRS for anorexic rabbits.

Oral suspensions are usually made up in tasty forms and can be given with oral syringes. Tablets can al- *Lefty's medicine slides right in from an oral syringe inserted into the side of his mouth (behind his teeth).* so be made tasty by crushing them into a teaspoon of mashed banana or applesauce. If your bunny refuses to lick it up from a dish, you can use an oral syringe with the tapered tip cut off. Drop the tablet, chopped or crushed, into the syringe and surround it with Nutrical, applesauce, or mashed banana.

The easiest way to give an uncooperative rabbit medicine is on the floor. Approach from behind a sleeping or relaxed rabbit. Straddle the rabbit. Kneel down with your feet turned in (so he can't back out between your legs). Put a hand on top of the head, with your thumb on the side of the mouth. Separate the lips with your thumb and stick the syringe in from the side. Easy enough.

If you and your bunny can't get down on the floor, you can lean over a table, tuck your bunny between one arm and your body, leaving your hand as

PHOTO: BOB HARRIMAN

free as possible. Use that hand to open the side of the mouth, and the other to insert the medicine.

Injections can be given from just about any position. Most rabbit injections are given at the tough insensitive area at the scruff, over the shoulders. Bunnies take injections quite well.

As you acquire medicines from your veterinarian, they will be specific to the illness being treated. Some medications can be kept for recurring illness, according to your veterinarian's instructions. Check expiration dates. At the same time that you stock your bunny's medicine cabinet with specific medications, you should have some general medical items on hand, such as:

Alcohol	*Oral syringes*	*Triple antibiotic*
Cotton swabs	*Petroleum jelly*	*ointment*
Gauze bandages	*Shaver/clippers*	*Vet-wrap*
Heating pad/disc	*Thermometer*	*Vinyl gloves*
Nebulizer	*(plastic)*	*Wound cleanser*

If you want to make the investment for home use with multiple animals, your veterinarian may train you to use an otoscope and stethoscope. ∎

First Aid but not Final Aid
By Mary Cotter, Ed.D.

DOES YOUR BUNNY:

1) Show no interest in food at all? *Take his temperature (normal is 101-103). If it's high (105 or above), gently cool him by wetting your hands with water (or alcohol) and stroking his ears. If it's low (below 99), warm him on a heating pad set on the lowest setting, with the cord fully protected so he cannot chew it. Alternatively, loosely fill a sock with rice, knot the top, and microwave briefly, to make a non-electric heating pad.*

Caution: Bunny skin burns easily! Never leave bunny unsupervised while he is on a heating pad! Do your best to get him to a bunny-savvy vet ASAP.

If your bunny approaches food and then moves away, or picks it up and then drops it, this could mean a tooth problem, which your vet can diagnose and treat ASAP.

2) Have loud gurgling sounds *coming from his belly? Does he keep repositioning himself, pressing his stomach to the floor? He may be trying to relieve gas pains. Give him a dose (around 1cc for most bunnies) of pediatric simethicone, and gently massage his belly,*

if he will tolerate it, using a flat-handed approach. For more information, see [http://fig.cox.miami.edu/Faculty/ Dana/ileus.html]

3) Have an injured or broken leg? *Most ER clinics can stabilize the bunny for you until you can see your regular bunny vet for full evaluation. Keep bunny in a small space to prevent jumping or excess movement on the leg until you can see your vet.*

4) have head tilt? *Is her head twisted around at an awkward angle? is she rolling? This condition be caused by an ear infection or a neurological problem (lesion in CNS). Create a carefully padded environment for her so she will not hurt herself until morning, when you can get to your vet. Hold her water bottle for her, and hand feed; many head tilt bunnies continue to have good appetites.*

5) have profuse and very watery diarrhea? *Dehydration can be life-threatening. Any ER clinic can administer fluids in an emergency.* ∎

Mary Cotter, Ed.D. *is the founder of* Rabbit Rescue and Rehab *of New York and producer of video,* Rabbit Handling and Nail Cutting

First Aid But Not Final Aid © 2005 by Mary Cotter.

Assisted Living

S PINAL INJURY OR DISEASE can leave a rabbit permanently disabled. Animals seem to have much less difficulty adjusting to loss of mobility than their humans do. Rabbits with crippling disease may stabilize and live comfortably and contentedly for a prolonged period of time.

Millions of humans are on lifelong medication, for everything from allergies to heart disease, and no one questions their quality of life. We don't destroy humans who are missing a limb or have a physical impairment. Many kinds of infirmity do not involve pain, so let's be careful about judging from appearances alone. If you have learned your rabbit's body language, you can sense a will to live.

Does he enjoy his meals? Does he enjoy being petted? Does he turn his ears towards intriguing sounds? Does he show an interest in the things going on around him? A successful program of assisted living depends on your bunny's attitude.

HABITATS FOR DISABILITIES

I make an effort to have habitats of disabled rabbits on a raised padded platform at a window level. This is so that I can reach them without too much stooping over and also to give them a view. Invariably immobile rabbits like to look out the window from a comfortable position. They appear to be entertained by birds and squirrels and even people doing yard work.

A floor option can also work for disabled bunnies in a padded section of a room and plenty of entertainment (i.e. toys and friends). The padding is to prevent pressure sores on any part of the body that is in constant contact with a hard surface. For bunnies who need to be propped up, roll up a brick in a small rug. Furnish habitats as follows:

Washable rugging   *Padded supports*
Flat Food bowl   *Water bottle*
Toys   *Companion*
Litterbox (maybe)   *A nice view*

FEEDING STRATEGIES

Some disabled rabbits are able to feed themselves. Most can drink more easily from a water bottle than from a bowl. Bunnies with disabilities should be enthusiastic eaters when their food is within reach. They can eat the same hay, veggies, and pellets that are good for ambulatory rabbits. Hand feeding may be necessary, at least part of the time (see page 59 for recipes).

A combination of feeding techniques can be used, by setting out less perishable produce and hay for while you are away, then give supplemental feedings in the evening when you are home.

PREVENTING URINE SCALD

Some semi-mobile bunnies can get into a litterbox that has a low entrance but still may be unable to "posture" (get into a position to project urine away from the body). Soaked fur on a disabled rabbit causes chapping and scalding. It's better to shave it off to keep the skin dry. You can have your veterinarian or veterinary assistant give your bunny a haircut or show you how to do it yourself. If the skin is badly inflamed, I use Neopredif powder or Sil-vadene ointment. When inflamation subsides, I just keep the area dry with baby powder (cornstarch).

For some bunnies, urine scald can only be prevented with diapers, which draw the moisture away from the tender flesh. Successful diapering is in the fit above the knees (keeping the knees out of the diaper). This is accomplished the way a seamstress shapes a sleeve—with slashes (step 3, below).

Every time you change the diaper, do the appropriate cleaning (page 87). But first check for those vitamin-packed cecotropes. If you have to separate them from the hard "marbles" to give to your bunny—well, wear your vinyl gloves.

SENIOR CARE

Bunnies who are in assisted living due to advanced age have their own set of additional needs. During the last two years of her life, my mother-in-law could tell me where she hurt and when she felt cold (nearly all the time). I learned from her that senior taste buds change, preferring junk food, and that self feeding becomes difficult. I noticed many similarities in my senior rabbits. If these bunnies were able to communicate their needs, these are some of the things they would tell us:

Warmth. Poor circulation makes me cold. If I can't exercise, keep my room warm, or give me a blanket.

Sleepy. I take lots of naps and may forget to eat.

My taste buds have changed, and I crave sweets (more fresh fruit, please).

Cushions keep me comfortable. Change my position frequently to prevent sores.

Stiff joints sometimes make me cranky. Don't forget my arthritis prescription.

Stress. I have low tolerance, so handle me gently.

Good sounds. I like to hear nice things. Talk to me, sing, and play my favorite music for me.

ACTIVITIES

Younger, more ambitious impaired rabbits can enjoy some independence and mobility with a cart to fit their size. Somewhat mobile bunnies may be more satisfied with a variety of toys to toss or cuddle, and, of course, continued interaction with companions.

Human interaction is also valuable. The feeling of simple petting is therapeutic. You can take up one of the touch modalities on page 53. And don't forget the visual and audial stimulus for those who like to gaze out the window and listen to music. ∎

Diaper preparation and fitting. These are the steps to adapting a human (newborn) diaper to a bunny's shape. Once the tail is through the tail-hole, place her front legs on a counter top, with hind legs down, while you attach the adhesive tabs in front. See page 79.

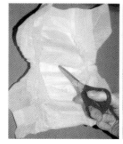 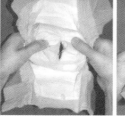  

1. Punch a tail hole in the middle with scissors.

2. Enlarge the slit to 2" or cut a diamond on the fold.

3. Slash the leg edges diagonally toward front.

4. Position bunny's tail to slide through the tail hole.

5. Dangle as a hammock to firmly "seat" the rump.

Care of the Young

Hand-raised orphans, from Hayward Animal Care and Control, await adoption.

WHENEVER I RECEIVE a frantic phone call over an "accidental" litter of babies, I always give a lecture on spaying and neutering. Rabbits can get pregnant the day they give birth!

Now let's assume the accident has already taken place. A young adolescent mother in a bewildered state has just dropped a bunch of babies behind your kitchen door. You're unprepared, and the stores are closed. What to do?

NECESSARY INGREDIENTS

A nestbox (about 12x14 inches). Cardboard will do temporarily, but it will get soggy and have to be replaced. The bottom should have a couple of drain holes. The sides can be about 8 inches high, but the front should be no higher than 4 inches where Mama Bunny enters and exits.

Bedding. Line the box with a 3-inch layer of clean yellow straw or finely shredded paper.

A fur-lined "well." Make a well with your fist in the middle of the nestbox and fill it with fur from the mother. If she hasn't pulled out fur herself, clip some.

Babies. Group them into this well of fur (yes, you can handle them). They will burrow to the bottom and stay there until Mother Bunny stands over them in her nursing postion.

Mama Bunny. Show her where her babies are but don't expect her to get in there with them. Rabbits nurse once a day—usually very late at night or pre-dawn. Rabbit milk is very rich in fat and protein and can sustain the babies for 24 hours. If you weigh the babies daily on a postal or kitchen scale and they are gaining weight, you can be sure that Mama Bunny is feeding them.

THE ORPHANED LITTER

Hand raising is very difficult. Yet we, and other rescuers, have taken in orphaned bunnies from animal shelters and raised them successfully, using slightly variations of the following basic techniques.

1. Set up a nestbox as described earlier, but instead of straw or paper, use very clean cotton baby blankets or soft t-shirts.

2. Provide warmth. Several babies brood each other (share body heat), but one or two may need help. Keep the room temperature at 70° day and night. You can attach a heating pad, on low setting, to one side of an open nestbox, but remember, this small area can overheat quickly. *Monitor closely.*

3. Sanitize. Wash your hands, before handling the babies, and sterilize feeding utensils.

"…a natural sucking motion closes the larynx and reduces the danger of aspiration."

4. Wash bunnies' faces and bottoms with warm water and cotton after every feeding. This is for cleanliness and also to help with elimination.

HAND FEEDING METHODS

You can bottle feed or syringe feed. Bottle feeding requires a perfect nipple. Carefully shave off some rubber at the end of the nipple. It's easier to punch the right size whole hole through thinner rubber. The hole should allow a fine spray (neither huge nor tiny drops). Once you get a perfect nipple, the babies' natural sucking motion closes the larynx and reduces the danger of aspiration.

With syringes the babies lap up the formula from the end of the syringe rather than draw with suction from a rubber nipple. Once started on syringes, they don't switch well to a bottle, because they lose their nursing reflex very quickly (within 2 days). Many wildlife rehabilitators prefer syringes, however, and feed only a few drops at a time to keep the liquid from entering the air passage. It does make sense to feed smaller amounts more often, since the formula is not as rich in fat and protein as mother's milk, and the babies become hungry more frequently.

WHAT TO FEED

Kitten or puppy formula can be used for rabbits. Some rehabbers enrich the formula with heavy cream (1/2–1cc). Various formulas, along with feeding and care techniques are offered on wildlife rehabilitation web sites. (see list on page 94).

Nearly all of my hand raised domestic rabbits survived on the feeding program in the following table. The usefulness of Lactobacillus acidophilus continues to be argued. These bacteria do not colonize in the rabbit intestine, but the lactic acid might

help keep the intestine sterile until healthy bacteria are introduced. I include it. These are the daily totals with gradual increases each week.

Age	KMR	Acidophilus
Newborn	5 cc	0.5 cc
1 week	15-25 cc	1 cc
2 weeks	25-27 cc	1 cc
3 weeks	30 cc	2 cc
4 weeks	30 cc	2 cc

Formula intake levels off around the 4th week, but continue to offer it in a dish. Orphans can follow the basic "beginner" diet on page 58. However, small amounts of baby food (squash, pumpkin, applesauce), offered in a dish at about 3 weeks, might provide a safer transition to non-sterile whole foods (at about 4 weeks). They should be eating dry alfalfa hay a few days before starting *clean* wet greens. ■

Grooming: the Ongoing Tune-up

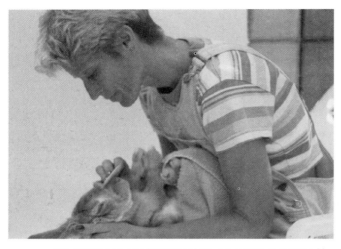

For shorter coats, a slicker brush is most commonly used for rabbits, although a rubber brush is useful during a shedding period to remove a lot of loose hair. I have come to use a flea comb for the major part of my rabbits' grooming. Flea combing is essential for elderly or disabled rabbits. It's not really the fleas that you're after, but rather the burrs and debris, and the potentially dangerous fly eggs (shown on page 75).

When using flea powders (carbaryl), as part of your bunny's weekly grooming routine, start at the neck and work downward separating about a one-inch section at a time. Work the powder in, all the way to the skin (not out into the air). For severe infestations of fleas or fur mites see page 75.

TOENAIL CLIPPING

When bunny's toenails grow too long, they catch in the carpeting or cage wire. Broken bleeding toenails are very prone to infection that can even invade bony tissue and cause serious damage. Always keep the toenails clipped short. Clip away the colorless part, being careful not to cut into the vein.

PHYSICAL MAINTENANCE OF YOUR RABBIT includes brushing, combing, manicuring, and cleaning. With regular grooming you can prevent several major health problems and save your bunny a trip to the veterinarian.

CARE OF THE COAT

Brushing or combing your rabbit keeps the coat clean and free of burrs, matts, and stickers. Brushing your rabbit will also remove loose hair that could otherwise build up in your vacuum cleaner, or worse yet in your rabbit's stomach. All rabbits shed to some extent, and most will go through major shedding a couple of times a year.

Long haired rabbits require daily brushing. If you're working with an extremely matted coat, you will need a matt splitter. Use a matt rake or matt splitter instead of scissors. Rabbits have delicate skin, which can be easily nicked and cut. If you must use scissors, get a blunt-nosed pair, and don't pull on the fur while you are trimming, or you may cut the skin. Keep the skin flat, and trim very patiently.

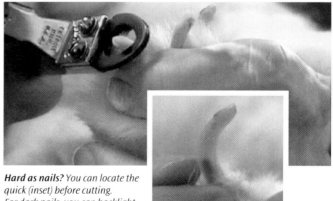

Hard as nails? *You can locate the quick (inset) before cutting. For dark nails, you can backlight them with a flashlight.*

"Choice cleaning methods keep the feet dry and wet fur to a minimum."

Have some styptic powder on hand. Do *not* even consider declawing your rabbit. There serious risk of infection. If your rabbit is digging the carpet, give her a large hay box and let her dig there instead.

EAR CLEANING

An otic chlorhexidine solution is good for dissolving waxy buildup in the ears, which can then be swabbed out with cotton. Be careful not to push wax further into the ear canal.

A dark crusty material in the ears is usually a sign of ear mite infestation. For treatment see page 74.

CLEANING THE HINDQUARTERS

Whether it's for ongoing hygiene or occasional problems with pasty stuck stool, dirty scent glands, or embedded debris, cleaning is necessary. Choice cleaning methods keep the feet dry and wet fur to a minimum.

Spot cleaning (middle). This is done seated (you) in a

Bunny Bidet

Spot Cleaning

chair. Roll bunny backwards with her head against your ribcage. Raise one leg to expose her underside. Then remove any burrs or foxtails that might have burrowed into the genital area.

Spray with a chlorhexidine cleansing solution, swab with cotton, then blot with tissue. If scent glands need cleaning, use cotton sticks.

Bunny bidet (upper right). Rather than dunking the hindquarters in water, slide bunny's bottom under a stream of running water from your bathroom or kitchen water spout, wetting just the "target" area. This is an ideal way to keep a diapered bunny clean.

Do it every time the diaper is changed and follow up with towel blotting and powdering.

Partial shower (left). This requires a spray nozzle attached to the water source. Spread a towel over part of a dish drainer in the sink. Place the disabled bunny's upper half on the towel. Shower off dirty areas—with minimal wetting and risk of shock. ∎

Partial Shower

The Well-Kept Rabbit

BY SANDI ACKERMAN

*T*he key to giving your rabbit the best chance for a long life, is to provide a happy environment and to spot problems early. Here are some life-extending procedures.

DAILY ROUTINES:

Hug your rabbit and as you do, become familiar with his body. You don't have to pick him up to do this, you can hug him while he and you are on the floor together. As you hug, feel him all over. Caress along his jaw line—then feel his tummy. Caress his head—then feel the crook of his legs and arms. Play "smushy face" with his entire head—then feel under his chin. You get the idea. Something that feels good—then something that may feel strange to him, at least the first few times you do this. He'll soon just think this is part of human behavior and will at first just put up with it but will soon learn to like this routine. What you are doing is getting used to the normal feel of his body, where his usual lumps and bumps are and how they feel on your healthy rabbit. Then, you'll be aware of any changes that might indicate a problem.

Check his litterbox looking for changes in the size or shape of his hard round droppings which can indicate an intestinal problem. Seeing some hair strung between droppings is normal when he's shedding, but if you see very thick hair between the droppings then you should read about hairballs again, just to make sure you're doing all that you can to help him pass the hair out of his stomach.

Touchy-feely: *Know the usual from the unusual*

And of course, make sure that he's been urinating. If you find very thick white or grey urine for more than a day or two, he may have too much calcium in his diet.

Bonding and grooming go together. In order to keep hair from flying around your home, and from being ingested by your rabbit, for just a couple of minutes every day comb or brush your rabbit. These short periods keeps the experience pleasant for both of you. Within a short time he will likely began to look forward to these few minutes of daily bonding.

Other daily tasks include supplying fresh water and pellets, fresh veggies and small amounts of fruit, and plenty of hay.

WEEKLY TASKS

Clean his living area thoroughly

Check eyes & nose to see that there is no discharge

Check inside ears to see if they look clean far down inside

EVERY OTHER MONTH

Clip nails

Check bottom of feet for sores

Check teeth to see that they're properly aligned

Clean genital scent glands (one on either side of the genitals)

Check scent gland under the chin. As rabbits age this area can become infected

Check for fleas

Check for dandruff (could be indicative of fur mites)

Keeping up with these health promoting tasks will mean a well kept rabbit. None of these things will take a lot of your time, but his time with you and the quality of both of your lives can be greatly increased. ∎

Sandi Ackerman is founder of Washington states' Best Little Rabbit, Rodent and Ferret House in Seattle and Rabbit Meadows Sanctuary in Redmond.

The Art of Caregiving

The better we can manage our time doing the mundane cleanup chores, the more quality-time we have to spend doing fun stuff with our bunnies.

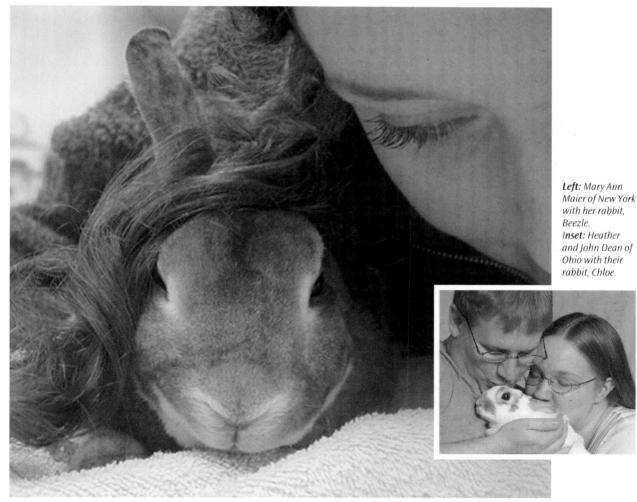

Left: *Mary Ann Maier of New York with her rabbit, Beezle.*
Inset: *Heather and John Dean of Ohio with their rabbit, Chloe.*

PHOTOS: ABOVE, COURTESY STAFF, CATNIP & CARROTS VETERINARY HOSPITAL; INSET, PENNEY ADAMS

More Rabbits: Less Work

MOST PEOPLE WHO ADOPT RABBITS come back to adopt again. A large part of the service of rescuers is to bond potential companions. As time goes on, multiple-rabbit households, which used to be the exception, are becoming the rule.

After a few years of managing multiple rabbits, we gain valuable experience, and most of us find housekeeping shortcuts and tips so that our best time is spent where it really counts—directly with

Supply corner:
Large stackable
containers are
used for hay and
litter. A long-
handled whisk
broom and
dustpan sweep
spilled hay.

the bunnies. We can spend those restful and refreshing hours grooming and petting our bunnies, and entertaining ourselves by watching their behavior. There are many good reasons to organize those other activities (called work) so that they don't take over our lives.

TOOLS AND EQUIPMENT AIDS

By the time you add bunnies to your household, you have already acquired general cleanup equipment—brooms, mops, vacuum cleaner. You also need to keep some convenient dedicated tools for the bunny area. These are my standard tools:

Containers. Large stackable plastic boxes with side openings are handy for storing pellets, hay, and litter.

Pick-up stick/grabber is useful for picking up small items that fall into inaccessible corners behind a habitat or for reaching an item on a high shelf without having to get the stepstool.

Short-handled whisk broom and dustpan are useful for counter-high areas and "reach-into" cages.

Long-handled whisk broom and dustpan are best for "step-inside" habitats and small floor areas.

Small hand-vacuum is obviously a versatile tool.

Atomizers (2) for white-vinegar spray. One is for cleaning the habitat area. The other is by the trash barrel where litterboxes are dumped and sprayed.

White vinegar (lots) prevents mineral build-up in litter boxes, and on habitat floors and wiring.

Scraper. This can be a putty knife, a paint scraper, or a curved linoleum cutter (my best all-purpose tool).

Sponges, rags, or paper towels.

Litter spatula/scooper. This is helpful only if fine-textured litter is used.

Bottle brush with large and small brush-ends. One end cleans the bottle; the other does the cap spout.

Scrub brush for occasional cleaning of habitat floor.

"Caregivers are often advised, 'Take care of yourself.' This ensures that you will be there for your bunnies for many years."

Regular vacuuming is necessary with any furry animal. Many people have rabbits in their (bunny-proofed) computer rooms. If you do this, keep a vacuum cleaner close by and use it frequently. Vacuum all around your computer, especially. It's amazing how much fly-around hair from cats, dogs, and rabbits can wind up inside your computer.

An occasional scattered "marble" can be swept up with a whisk broom or hand vacuum. For urine accidents on carpeting, upholstery, or bedspreads, use white vinegar, the all-purpose cleaner for rabbit environments. It is nontoxic to rabbits while it discourages the growth of bacteria. Rabbit urine is highly alkaline. The acidity of vinegar neutralizes the alkaline and works for cleaning rabbit urine.

ADAPT THE ENVIRONMENT

Management of my own multiple-rabbit household will undoubtedly continue to change, as it has for the past 20 years. I am constantly upgrading my cleaning aids, looking for new time-saving devices, and remodeling living space to minimize my work.

At one time I insisted that everyone drop to the floor to attend to their bunnies. This demand was unrealistic for people with disabilities or just the discomforts of aging. Ramps to upper levels can bring bunny to you when it's not easy to do extensive work on the floor. In my own advancing years, I can still get up and down without difficulty, but I don't enjoy stepping over baby fencing. I now want baby gates that swing open. With my custom constructed habitats, I simply remove the front door and step into the habitat but not over the fence.

Another advantage to large, walk-in habitats is that they eliminate the strain of kneeling at the door and reaching inside to clean them. I just go inside and sit down on the habitat floor. All corners and alcoves are within reach for cleaning.

My crippled rabbits, of course, live on elevated

Whisk broom for all: Frannie and Zooey find anther use for their human's handy cleaning tool.

platforms at my standing level, where I can have quick and easy access to the bunnies themselves.

I empty litterboxes one at a time (much less strenuous, avoiding aching shoulders and back). I find it easier to make many trips to the trash barrel on the service porch with one lightweight box, rather than one trip, loaded to my chin with the heavy weight of multiple boxes.

TAKING A BREAK

Caregivers are often advised, "Take care of yourself." This ensures that you will be there for your bunnies for many years. This advice includes getting away for a vacation or a weekend outing. Going away, however, is of no use at all if you take all your worries with you. The best thing you can do is to line up a good pet-sitter so that you can take a break when you need to.

Obviously, your first choice is to ask close friends who already know your rabbit to look after him in your absence. The better your friends know

PHOTO: AMY ESPIE

your rabbit the easier it will be for everyone. But if you live alone in a new area, you may not yet have friends nearby.

The next best thing to having a bunny-sitter who knows your rabbit is to have one who knows rabbits. You may want to start by asking your vet for referrals for either a reputable boarding kennel or a pet-sitting service. A variety of services are available. A veterinary bulletin board is a place to look for a pet-sitter. Check on what suits your needs best. Some do actual house-sitting. Others will come in at specified times to feed and exercise your animals. Others may board your animal on their own premises. If you choose boarding, you will of course want to see the facilities. Check for kennel cleanliness and ask about exercise accommodations.

Competent pet-sitters are familiar with health needs of the species that they're working with. Most are experienced at giving injections and can follow any program that your veterinarian has prescribed.

Many humane societies and veterinary hospitals also offer boarding with varying degrees of exercise available. A printout of your bunnies' histories and schedules (detailed on page 93), as well as diet requirements, will ensure that your bunny receives the same quality of care in your absence. Your policy, if your bunny-sitter doesn't already require it, should include instructions for emergency care and a check made out to your veterinarian. With as many needs as possible anticipated in advance, you will have a much more relaxing time away.

NETWORKING WITH OTHER RABBIT PEOPLE

One of the many positive changes that have taken place since the first edition of *House Rabbit Handbook* is that you can say with certainty that you are not alone. There was a time when rabbit information was limited to breeding or laboratory settings. We had to build on our experience with rabbits as house companions and share the information with each other. Rabbit care and behavior information is now available in abundance online. Just browse around.

Concerned volunteers Janice Tunder and Karen Johanson check a boarding bunny's ears at the HRS Rabbit Center. Many shelters and veterinary facilities offer high-quality boarding care.

You can go to www.rabbit.org. and follow the links to a local House Rabbit Society chapter or other rescue organization near you, or you can join one or many of the chat lists available to discuss behavior and health issues.

You can exchange ideas and meet other rabbit people from all parts of the world. You don't even have to be physically close, unless you need to share bunny-sitting or participate in volunteer activities. The best part is that you will find many people who will support you in your compulsion to love a bunny. ∎

Health Records for Peace of Mind

UNLESS YOU PARTICIPATE in an online database and share photo albums, the one thing you won't find on the Internet is your rabbit's history. Building your bunny's history is your job. By shooting photos and video, you are already documenting behavior at certain ages. By adding your comments and observations and items from your veterinary records you create your bunny's history.

Your bunny's history may save another bunny's life or even his own life at some point in the future. For many years the House Rabbit Society has been compiling health data from rabbits in foster homes and adoptive homes for the purpose of helping veterinarians to compare and diagnose similar problems in rabbits. You can contribute to this or a similar public database, or you can keep your own desktop database. If you don't have database software, a simple spreadsheet will do.

Start with your bunny's physical data. Assign an ID number since you may have more than one bunny throughout your lifetime. Include a birthdate even if it has to be estimated. Then every time you visit the vet, get a copy of the exam record or summarize the major parts: the problem or "chief complaint" (which you have already given as the reason for the appointment), the assessment (what the doctor observes), and a diagnosis. Sometimes the diagnosis (dx) will be a preliminary or "differential" diagnosis (ddx) until test results come in.

You can store your records in a paper file, or transcribe them into an electronic database. Either way it's good to have some paper on hand in case you have to rush to an emergency clinic during the night and your file is the only health record available at the time. Even if you don't get to an emergency clinic the night before, it is still very helpful to your own veterinarian to see your record of what you did to help your sick bunny. My home health care files

Keeping up appearances: *Fiona's face-washing routine is part of the daily life of a fastidious lady.*

include date, time, bunny's temperature, what first-aid treatment was given and response. This saves valuable time, and my veterinarian clips my home sheet right into her hospital record. After a long time gap between my bunnies' illnesses, I am prone to forget many little helpful tips I learned from their previous episodes. Then I am ever so grateful that I have kept their records.

TRUST NOT TO MEMORY

Even if you don't keep health records, a simple routine-behavior schedule is helpful to have on paper in a visible place. The main reason to do this is that the human mind can become preoccupied—with problems from work or the anticipation of weekend guests, or any number of life's stresses. These are the times not to rely on your memory but instead just to go down the list so that you don't have to think. Have your list ask you, Did they eat their favorite treats? Are they passing normal "pills"? Are they grooming themselves? Is the water bottle empty? Under normal circumstances you don't need reminders, but bunnies get sick at the most inopportune times. I know this from my bunnies' history,

So the rule is to be especially vigilant when you have the least time. It will save you more time in the long run and free you from worrying about oversights. When you know all is well with your bunnies, you will enjoy your other activities more. ■

Notes

REFERENCES

Buddington, R. and J. Diamond. 1990. Ontogenetic development of monosaccharide and amino acid transporters in rabbit intestine. *American Journal of Physiology* 259:G544-55

Brown, Susan A. Hairballs in Rabbits:Fact or Fiction, April 1996, <http://www.hrschicago.org/ hairballfr.html> (January 2005).

Cheeke, P.R. 1987. *Rabbit Feeding and Nutrition.* Orlando: Academic Press

Deeb, Barbara (2002) Cardiovascular disease in rabbits. *House Rabbit Journal* 3: 8,9

Fraga, M. 1990. Effect of type of fibre on the rate of passage and on the contribution of soft feces to nutrient intake of finishing rabbits. Journal of Animal Science 69:1566-74

Gidenne, T. 1992. Effect of fibre level, particle size and adaptation period on digestibility and rate of passage as measured at the ileum and in the faeces in the adult rabbit. British Journal of Nutrition. 67: 133-46

Lebas, F. (1980). Les recherches sur l'alimentation du lapin: Evolution au cours de 20 dernieres annees et perspectives d'avenir. Adapted by P. Cheeke1987. *Rabbit Feeding and Nutrition.* Academic Press

Perch, D.H. and S.W. Barthold. 1993. Pp. 179-80 in *Pathology of Laboratory Rodents and Rabbits* Ames, IA: Iowa State University Press

Sakaguchi, E. 1990. Digesta retention and fibre digestion in brushtail possums, ringtail possums and rabbits. Comparative Biochemistry and Physiology 96A:351-54

Wagner, J.L. 1974. Spontaneous deaths in rabbits resulting from gastric trichobezoars. Laboratory Animal Science 24:826-30

RECOMMENDED READING

Books

The Biology and Medicine of Rabbits and Rodents
By John E. Harkness and Joseph E. Wagner,

A Practitioner's Guide to Rabbits and Ferrets
By Jeffrey R. Jenkins, D.V.M. and Susan Brown, D.V.M.

Ferrets, Rabbits Rodents
By Katherine E. Quesenberry and James W. Carpenter

The Relaxed Rabbit: Massage for Your Pet Bunny
By Chandra Moira Beal

Why Does My Rabbit...?
By Anne McBride

Rabbit Health in the 21st Century
By Kathy Smith

When Only the Love Remains
By Emily Stuparyk

Pamphlets (walk in and pick up)

HOUSE RABBIT SOCIETY (HRS) national headquarters
148 Broadway, Richmond, CA 94804. 510-970-7575.

YOUR LOCAL HUMANE SOCIETY OR SPCA

YOUR VETERINARIAN'S OFFICE

On-Line

<http://www.rabbit.org>
General care, archives, and links to chapter and other rabbit rescue web pages

<http://www.hrschicago.org/articles>
A vast array of comprehensive health articles by Susan A. Brown, D.V.M.

<http://www.rabbit.org/chapters/san-diego/health/index.html> Archived newsletters include various articles by Jeffrey R. Jenkins, D.V.M.

<http://www.WisconsinHRS.org/Care>
Newsletter archives include "Declawing Rabbits" [reasons not to] by Joanne Paul-Murphy, D.V.M.

< http://fig.cox.miami.edu/Faculty/Dana/ileus>
"GastroIntestinal Stasis, The Silent Killer" by Dana M. Krempels, Ph.D.

<http://www.squirrelworld.com/RabRehab>
"Successful Wild Baby Rabbit Care/Rehabilitation" by Lou Rea Kenyon

<http://www.2ndchance.info/bunnies>
"Caring for Orphan Wild Bunnies" by R.S. Hines D.V.M., Ph.D.

<http://www.catsandrabbitsandmore.com>
"Bijou" Caring for a Disabled Rabbit by Amy Spintman

<http://home.kc.rr.com/jhabernal/mohrskc/hrswebpg19>
"Paresis/Paralysis" by Kim Clevenger
"Tribute to Tiffy" by Terry Clevenger

<http://ohare.org/specials.htm#finn>
"Spotlight on Finn" by Kristen Doherty

EMERCENCY

Your local after-hours emergency clinic

ASPCA animal poison control center

For any animal poison-related emergency, (888) 426-4435.

Index